D1553164

THE GREAT DEBATE

THE GREAT DEBATE

Theories of Nuclear Strategy

Raymond Aron

Translated from the French by
Ernst Pawel

UNIVERSITY
PRESS OF
AMERICA

LANHAM • NEW YORK • LONDON

University Press of America,® Inc.

4720 Boston Way
Lanham, MD 20706

This edition was reprinted in 1985 by University Press of America,® Inc. by
arrangement with Doubleday & Company, Inc.

Library of Congress Cataloging in Publication Data

Aron, Raymond, 1905-
  The great debate.

  Translation of: Le grand débate.
  Reprint. Previously published: Garden City, N.Y.:
Doubleday, 1965. With new introd.
  Includes bibliographical references.
  1. Strategy. 2. Nuclear warfare. 3. World
politics—1945-   . I. Title.
U163.A7413 1985   355'.0217   85-7271
ISBN 0-8191-4564-5 (pbk. : alk. paper)

Preface to the American Edition

During the academic year 1962–63, I gave a course
at the *Institut d'Etudes Politiques* at the University of
Paris, the subject of which was the influence of modern armaments on international relations. This basic
course on atomic strategy was the first of its kind in
France, and while I was giving it, the debate about
what the newspapers called the "striking force" and
the official documents referred to as the "strategic nuclear force" was going on, within France and between
France and its allies. This book grew out of my lec-
tures, which I rewrote during the summer of 1963; in
the spring of 1964 I reread and revised it for the English translation.

It may be useful to repeat here the reasons with
which I convinced my French audience that a social
scientist, trained in philosophy, can legitimately take
an interest in the problems, at once traditional and
unprecedented, that nuclear weapons pose for governments and for humanity in general.

In the teaching of political science and history, the
study of military institutions and their relationship to
nations or societies ought to be emphasized more than
they usually are. To stress primarily descriptions of

battles is deplorable; reasonable men cannot forget that wars have been, throughout history, an endemic phenomenon, and that weapons, like the tools of laborers, are at the same time the reflection of a society and one of the factors that shape it. Moreover, in a democracy, national defense is the concern of each citizen. Is it not the duty of the individual citizen to learn enough at least to understand the problems? In this respect, what is important in economic affairs is no less necessary in matters of strategy.

In the old days, before 1914 or even before 1939, military plans, hidden in the files of general staffs, were never openly discussed in print, at least not by non-specialists. The generals prepared for war in time of peace, but civilians never confused the two. Today this is no longer so. The less likely it seems that these monstrous weapons will be used, the more diplomats, political figures and journalists discuss them. The strategy known as deterrence is, in essence, a form of diplomacy, because it aims to prevent certain moves by nations believed to be hostile by threatening them with military retaliation. Diplomacy has always been intended to influence adversaries or partners, allies or enemies, to do certain things and to refrain from doing others. The menace of enemy countries has always been implicit in the idea of international relations. But never before has the danger been so huge, and the deterrence so continuous and organized; never before have unused weapons weighed so heavily, if not upon the course of events, at least upon the discussions among nations. It is as if the non-use of these weapons for military purposes were inseparable from their continuous use for diplomatic ends. For a nation to be able to avoid using them, it must make other nations believe that it will do so in certain circumstances.

Nuclear weapons have accentuated one aspect of international relations that is not entirely new. I shall call it the *polymorphism of armed conflicts*. In every epoch, conflicts between political units have recurred in different forms, and according to the size of the units involved and the importance of the stakes, the coefficient of mobilization and the violence of the fighting varied. Now a fundamental distinction has been introduced, the distinction between conventional and atomic weapons. This raises three major questions: in what circumstances would the latter be used, what are the chances of avoiding their use in case of local hostilities, and what are the risks of escalation from one type of arms to another?

Finally, let me recall to the reader two well-known *bons mots*, attributed to two famous Frenchmen. "War," said Clemenceau, "is too serious a matter to be left to the generals." But when former British Prime Minister Clement Attlee wrote, in an article on General de Gaulle's memoirs, that the leader of the Free French was a great general but a bad politician, the general replied, "Politics is too serious a matter to be left to the politicians."

Both statements seem to me equally incontestable. The only way to reconcile them—or to try to do so—is to give military men a political training and to insist that policy makers be acquainted with at least the foundations of strategy, if not with the practical aspects of the art of war.

In the United States, the number of books and articles devoted to the problems I shall consider in this

little volume is considerable, and I gladly acknowledge my debt to these American authors. But perhaps
even in the United States my contribution to the discussion may not be completely valueless, for two main
reasons.

Each American strategist has his own doctrine.
None has taken the trouble to explain the way of
thinking common to all of them. Perhaps none of
them will give his unqualified approval to my synopsis
of their methods of analysis and reasoning. But in
spite of this—and even because of it—they may derive
some benefit from reading my interpretation of their
strategic theories, if only because it inspires further
discussion of the subject.

Besides, although I do not subscribe to all the criti-
cisms of the American theories that many Europeans
have voiced, I shall at least try to make these criti-
cisms intelligible to Americans and to isolate the grains
of truth and rationality, military and psychological,
that they contain. For those who hope for the survival
of the Atlantic Alliance, it is of primary importance
that the policy makers and the public on either side of
the Atlantic gain a greater understanding of the positions held on the other side.

In 1962–63 Europeans and Americans were passionately debating questions of strategy; today, because of the international thaw and the rapprochement between the United States and the Soviet Union,
the discussion has died down. But any unforeseen
change in the international situation could revive it
tomorrow, and in any circumstances, having once discovered them, mankind can never forget the secrets
of the atom. Diplomatic constellations will change, but

the goal will remain the same: until the world is truly peaceful and disarmament a reality, nations must learn the art of using thermonuclear weapons on the diplomatic level in such a way that they will never have to use them on the military level.

No one can claim to know all the subtleties of that art, but everyone must learn the rudiments of it.

Contents

1

Fifteen Years of Technological Revolution,
1945–60

So far, only two atom bombs have been used in actual military operations. Those two—the total number in existence at the time—were dropped from American planes and exploded at low altitude. They devastated two Japanese cities.

This is an account of the first atomic explosion, which hit Hiroshima on August 6, 1945, at 8:15 A.M., as quoted in a special U. S. Air Force report:[1]

Most of the industrial workers had already reported to work, but many workers were en route and nearly all school children and some industrial employes were at work outdoors on the program of building removal to provide firebreaks and disperse valuables to the country. The attack came forty-five minutes after the "all clear" had been sounded from a previous alert. Because of the lack of warning and the populace's indifference to small groups of planes, the explosion came as an almost complete surprise and the people had not taken shelter. Many were in the open, and most of the rest in flimsily constructed homes or commercial establishments. . . . The surprise, the collapse of many buildings, and the conflagration con-

[1] U. S. Strategic Bombing Survey 4 & 5, Washington, 1946, as cited by P. M. S. Blackett, *Fear, War and the Bomb*, New York, 1949, p. 39.

tributed to an unprecedented casualty rate. Seventy
to eighty thousand people were killed, or missing and
presumed dead, and nearly as many were injured.
The magnitude of the casualties is set in relief by a
comparison with the Tokyo raid of March 9–10, 1945,
in which, though nearly sixteen square miles were
destroyed, the number killed was no greater. . . .

At Nagasaki, three days later, the city was scarcely
more prepared, though vague reference to the Hiroshima disaster had appeared in the newspapers of
August 8.

The following table, extracted from U.S.S.B.S. 5,
summarizes the comparative effects of the Hiroshima
and Nagasaki bombs as against 1667 tons of conventional bombs:

Effort and Results	Hiroshima	Nagasaki	Tokyo	Average of 93 Urban Attacks
Planes	1	1	279	
Bomb load	Atomic bomb	Atomic bomb	1,667 tons normal bombs	1,129 tons normal bombs
Population density per square mile	35,000	65,000	130,000	
Square miles destroyed	4.7	1.8	15.8	1.8
Killed and missing	70–80,000	35–40,000	83,600	1,850
Injured	70,000	40,000	102,000	1,830
Mortality rate per square mile destroyed	15,000	20,000	5,300	1,000
Casualty rate per square mile	32,000	43,000	11,800	2,000

In 1949 when he wrote *Fear, War, and the Bomb*,
P. M. S. Blackett, a Nobel Prize winner in physics,
tried to emphasize the limitations rather than the

scope of the military revolution brought about by nuclear explosives. The explosive power of the Hiroshima and Nagasaki plutonium bombs equaled 20,000 tons of TNT; but, on the basis of figures published by U. S. experts, he calculated that the actual damage produced by a 20-kiloton bomb was equal to only 2000 tons of conventional explosives. A U. S. survey rated the 20-kiloton plutonium bomb as equivalent to 167 "blockbusters" or 10-ton bombs containing 5 tons of TNT each. The huge loss of life at Hiroshima and Nagasaki was at least partly due to the surprise nature of the attack, which caught the population out in the open.

In 1949 it was still possible to maintain that a few dozen or even a few hundred atom bombs would not decide the ultimate outcome of a war; but production of the thermonuclear bomb put an end to all such speculation. In 1944 the Allies dropped a total of 600,000 tons of bombs on Germany or the equivalent of three hundred A-bombs, if one 20-kiloton A-bomb equals 2000 tons, in spite of which German tank and airplane production continued to increase. The energy yield of a single thermonuclear bomb, however, is figured in millions rather than thousands of tons of TNT; in other words, the explosive power of one such bomb exceeds the total of all the bombs dropped on Germany in the course of World War II, whatever mathematical corrections can be made because destruction does not increase in direct ratio to explosive power. There is no escaping the fact that the new weapon has brought about quantitative changes so vast that they amount to a qualitative revolution.

The effects of nuclear explosion are *mechanical, thermal and radioactive.*[2]

> Mechanical effects, i.e., blast, caused damage classified as "severe" (complete destruction of brick buildings several stories high, severe damage to metal construction) at 1.2 miles from Ground Zero at Hiroshima. . . . The formula giving the range of damage as proportional to the cubic root of the energy yield makes possible calculations of explosive power. Thus following the test explosion of March 1, 1954, estimated in the 20-megaton range, the Atomic Energy Commission gave the range of severe blast damage as 11.25 miles, i.e., ten times that of Hiroshima, where 20 kilotons—one-thousandth the energy—were exploded. . . . *An explosive charge of this order is sufficient to effect total destruction of the largest cities, even if the range of destruction is reduced to 10.5 miles in accordance with the revised estimates of 1957.*[3]

The thermal effects present complex problems, for which I refer to M. Rougeron's book. He deals in detail with the two U. S. manuals of 1950 and 1957, and I am here merely summarizing his conclusions. The risk of conflagration depends upon a multiplicity of factors; but the attenuation of thermal effects in proportion to distance determines the efficiency of different types of bombs and the altitude at which they are exploded. According to an earlier formula, "the number of calories received per unit of surface decreases in geometric progression as the distance increases in arithmetic progression, thus following a so-called 'exponential' law wholly different from previous laws of

[2] Camille Rougeron: *La Guerre Nucléaire,* Paris, Calmann-Lévy, 1962.
[3] Rougeron, op. cit., p. 40.

the square or cubic root of distance." But in the 1957 handbook this exponential law was replaced by a formula of decrease considerably less drastic as regards large distances. "A comparison in figures will indicate the difference between the 1950 and the 1957 laws on retained absorption; for a 20 kiloton charge in average clear weather, a target at 6.25 miles from the explosion would receive 0.01 calories per square centimeter according to the earlier formula, and 0.3 cal/cm², i.e., thirty times as much, according to the later one."[4]

Since 1955 M. Rougeron has been stressing the incendiary effects of high-altitude bursts. "The demonstration was based on the absorption law as postulated in 1950; the experimental observations that resulted in the 1957 revisions tend only to lend further support to the conclusions. The thermal effect is greatest in a high altitude burst; this alone allows it full benefit of the law of diffusion according to the square root of the distance, which in the first approximation guarantees the constancy of incendiary destruction yield regardless of the force of the explosion. . . . Increasing the altitude tends to reduce absorption at a rate much higher than that resulting from a single absorption of density. . . . At an altitude of 15.5 miles, the intensity of thermal radiation is 2.4 times greater than in a low-level burst of the same power."[5]

At a press conference on October 1, 1961, a representative of the Atomic Energy Commission evaluated the effects of a 100-megaton (one hundred *million* tons of TNT) explosion as follows: "Major blast damage would range out to about 18 miles from

[4] Rougeron, op. cit., pp. 45–47.
[5] Idem, pp. 48–49.

`Ground Zero and cover 1,080 square miles, figures somewhere in between those of 1950 and 1957; but as to fire, extending up to nearly 60 miles and covering an 11,300 square mile area, almost 2,000 square miles larger than the state of Vermont, the conclusions of those two handbooks have been scrapped completely."

M. Rougeron does not stop there; he has thought of other ways to enlarge the area of destruction. "Simultaneous ultra-high level bursts are an ultimate means of compounding their incendiary effects." Thus it seems at least conceivable that by exploding very powerful bombs at very high altitudes (fifteen to twenty miles) in order to reduce atmospheric absorption and increase the emission of thermal flux at the expense of blast, fires can be started that will cover areas measuring thousands of square miles.[6]

The effects of radiation, both immediate and delayed, again depend on a large number of factors. Radioactive fallout varies according to the altitude of the burst and the type of bomb ("clean" or "dirty," to use terms hallowed by usage). In high-altitude explosions the neutrons are not captured and thus act over great distances, while near-ground-level bursts raise radioactive debris that can cause death hundreds of miles from Ground Zero. In the event of a thermonuclear war the atmosphere would remain polluted for days or even weeks, so that survival would be possible only in underground shelters.

The sole purpose of this brief survey is a reminder, before I begin to discuss strategy, of the almost inconceivable horror implicit in the notion of a total war

[6] See below, pp. 245–46.

fought with the thermonuclear weapons now available. A single bomb of a few megatons will wipe out a large city. Radiation can kill over distances hundreds of miles from the site of the explosion and weeks after it takes place, while hundreds or even thousands of square miles would be reduced to ashes by super-bombs exploded at high altitudes.[7]

It does not follow that total war would put an end to the human adventure; unleashed today, it would leave survivors even in the countries most directly affected. Inevitably those would be the countries possessing nuclear arms; since they also happen to be the most advanced industrially and hence the very ones whose resources would be most desperately needed in the task of later reconstruction, we can get an idea of the monstrous folly involved in a life-and-death conflict between the Big Two. We can also understand the salutary complicity that now links them in their efforts to avoid a thermonuclear apocalypse.

The step from the atomic to the thermonuclear bomb was at least as radical as that from so-called conventional chemical explosives to atomic (or fission) bombs; some, in fact, date the *qualitative* revolution from the advent of the H-bomb rather than the A-bomb.

But two other milestones were also passed along the way. The first was *miniaturization*. The Big Two have bombs in the 10-megaton range, but at the same time they have developed bombs and shells whose explo-

---

[7] M. Rougeron accuses me of overestimating the effect of the new weapons; anyone familiar with his books will appreciate the sense of humor revealed by this accusation.

sive yield is well below that of the 20-kiloton Hiroshima or Nagasaki models.

There is now a linear continuity in explosive power. It may be that the most powerful conventional weapons are or will be more powerful than the least powerful atomic weapons. Because nuclear warheads can be fitted to infantry weapons, some people have therefore inferred that it is now impossible to make distinctions between nuclear and conventional arms, at least for members of the nuclear club. This conclusion is not at all obvious. It is true, however, that the development of so-called tactical nuclear weapons, i.e., weapons that can be used on the battlefield by soldiers in the line, makes it more difficult to limit hostilities and that escalation, once troops equipped with such weapons are engaged, is more to be feared.

The diversification of the atomic arsenal aiming simultaneously at the ever-larger and the ever-smaller depended on an increase in the available quantities of fissionable material. In 1949 the scientific advisers of the U. S. Atomic Energy Commission were reluctant to recommend production of the H-bomb; the dissipation of scarce resources on behalf of a project whose outcome seemed uncertain constituted one of the major arguments against it. Today scarcity is no longer a problem; in fact, since production for military purposes has been curtailed, the United States has an abundance of fissionable material. The number of bombs and nuclear or atomic warheads in the United States today is estimated at something like 50,000; Russian stockpiles, though smaller, are nonetheless substantial (several thousand).

The improvement in the means of delivery has

matched that of the weapons themselves. The two types presently available are planes and ballistic missiles. As regards planes, progress in one direction has resulted in bombers capable of carrying huge loads over great distances (better than 6250 miles), flying at altitudes of above 45,000 feet and reaching any target in the Soviet Union from bases located in the United States. At the same time fighters or fighter-bombers capable of carrying A-bombs—if not H-bombs —at supersonic speeds have been developed, and vertical-take-off planes are already in the test stage.

What really revolutionized the means of delivery, however, was neither supersonic speeds nor heavy bombers, but ballistic missiles. If the H-bomb revolutionized energy, the ballistic missile revolutionized time. The four to five thousand miles separating missile base from target can now be traversed in about half an hour. Even granting the most efficient satellite warning system possible, a chief of state will have only minutes in which to make his decisions once he learns that one or more ballistic missiles have been launched.

When, precisely, did these various revolutions take place?

During the first five years of the atomic age the United States held a monopoly; this ended in 1949, when the Soviet Union exploded its first atom bomb. But by 1950, when the Korean War broke out, the United States had clearly not yet reached the point of either nuclear abundance or miniaturization. Thermonuclear bombs were first tested more or less simultaneously by both Russia and the United States, at the close of the decade. Ten years after Hiroshima and Nagasaki scarcity of fissionable material had become a

thing of the past as far as the Big Two were concerned; tactical arms, if not already available to combat units, were at least in the planning stage; and
thermonuclear bombs had been produced. At the end
of the next five years both sides had ballistic missiles
ready on their launching pads, some with an intermediate range of between 1200 and 2000 miles, others
—still few in number—intercontinental missiles with a
range of from 5000 to 6000 miles. In 1963 we entered
the fourth five-year cycle, which is marked by a rapid
increase in the number of ballistic missiles as well as
by dissension within both the Atlantic Alliance and
the Soviet bloc, arising from the monopoly or quasi-
monopoly of nuclear arms that the leading nation on
each side, East and West, is determined to keep.

This brief summary of the technological revolutions
cannot claim to convey even an approximate idea of
the arms race over the past fifteen years. This race
can be understood only by tracing the whole series of
challenges and responses—the means of aggression acquired by one side and the means of defense mounted
by the other in return. Both sides, of course, have aggressive as well as defensive weapons on both the
strategic and tactical levels. The Red Army was the
answer to the American atom bomb on the political
and strategic level, and the stepped-up production of
fighter planes was the Russian response to the B-36,
B-47 or B-52 on the tactical level.[8] All I am trying to

[8] I do not intend to suggest that all decisions on arms systems
on either side were rational, according to the present judgment
of the experts. In Moscow as in Washington, the pressures from
the different services and the vague feelings of political leaders
may have had as much influence as the strategic reasoning.

do in distinguishing the successive cycles within this fifteen-year period is to relate the nuclear balance to the course of diplomatic activity. Such comparison should enable us to gauge the influence exerted by arms in general, and nuclear arms in particular, on international relations.

The years from 1945 to 1950 were the era of the American monopoly, but a monopoly confined to the A-bomb, which was still in short supply. The United States had no small tactical weapons suitable for battlefield use, and A-bombs themselves were still sufficiently rare to be reserved for targets deemed worth the huge investment. Delivery depended on bombers, among them the long-range B-36, which could deliver great weights but was concentrated at a few airports in the United States. But by 1953 the atomic shortage had apparently eased to the point where John Foster Dulles' threat to resort to nuclear arms, transmitted to Peking via New Delhi, was anything but a bluff.

Throughout the second phase, from 1950 to 1957, while the Big Two both had thermonuclear bombs,[9] the United States retained a substantial twofold lead. It was ahead in the miniaturization of atomic arms, and therefore in their adaptation for potential use on the battlefield, and it had a strategic air force superior in numbers, equipment, and training to its Soviet counterpart. Furthermore, the United States had ringed its rival's territory with a belt of air bases from which medium or fighter bombers could strike at most of the places designated as targets in the event of all-out war—not to mention aircraft carriers. All the fac-

[9] First tests in 1953.

tors making for this United States superiority were
still fully operative as late as 1956, that is, at the time
of the Hungarian revolution. Russia's strategic bombers, imitations of United States models to begin with,
were few in number (100 to 200), vulnerably exposed
on the ground, and, in any case, incapable of inflicting
upon American cities anything comparable to the devastation that would have been visited upon Soviet
territory.

The start of a new phase may be reckoned from the
launching of the first Soviet sputnik in October 1957.
Actually, the threat to the American mainland did not
immediately increase to any decisive degree. Between
1958 and 1960 the Soviets seem to have concentrated
on the production of medium-range rather than intercontinental ballistic missiles, if United States estimates
of 50 to 100 Soviet ICBMs as of January 1963 are accurate.[10] But the psychological effect of the apparent
Russian head start in missile development (the thrust
of rocket engines, to be precise) and space explora-
tion was out of all proportion to any actual shift in
the relative balance of power.

There are several reasons to account for what Europeans, spokesmen for "uncommitted nations" (who
are fond of considering themselves mere onlookers)
and even some American leaders viewed as a deteri-
oration of the former balance of nuclear power between the United States and Russia. First, the Atlantic
Alliance, which consists of two sectors—the western
edge of the Asian-European land mass and the Ameri-

[10] The same threat that the hundreds of MRBMs meant to
Western Europe had existed before, during the period of the
Red Army's great superiority.

can mainland several thousand miles to the west—had always been able to take for granted the invulnerability (or very minimal vulnerability once the Soviet strategic air force had come into existence) of United States territory. The mainland of the leading country in the alliance, the protector of the weaker and more exposed members, was beyond the enemy's reach. But now it suddenly appeared that if Russia either acquired more intercontinental missiles than the United States or produced them before the United States could do so, the American mainland would be more vulnerable even than Russian territory. In reality this would have held true only if the superiority of the United States strategic air force had abruptly ceased to weigh in the balance; but the mere fact that the number of Soviet missiles able to hit United States targets from Russian bases was said to be greater than the number of American missiles that could be launched in the opposite direction assumed a symbolic significance and seemed to usher in a shift in relative positions.

Second, United States leaders, military as well as civilian, exacerbated the impact of events by asking their allies to let America construct, on their respective territories, launching ramps for medium-range ballistic missiles—15 Jupiters in Turkey, 30 Thors in Italy, and 60 Thors in Great Britain.[11] This tended to make it appear that one side had intercontinental missiles and the other only medium-range ones, and that the United States, in order to restore the balance of deterrence, would need help from the very allies whose

[11] France received and rejected the same offer or request.

`protector it had been in the preceding phase. For while overseas bases had been in operation all along, the main deterrent (SAC) was kept on the far side of the Atlantic.

Finally, there was the argument about the missile gap that broke out in the United States. In 1958 this famous gap was predicted for 1960 or 1961, and by 1959 it had receded to 1962 or 1963, but it certainly gave rise to fears of a Soviet lead—at least relative— within the not-too-distant, if ill-defined future. The West did not stop to reflect on the long years of very clear Soviet inferiority vis-à-vis the United States and on the fact that this inferiority had seemed to cause the Russians very little trouble; the end of a previously incontrovertible superiority or the incipient reversal in relative strength seemed fraught with danger.

It is true, of course, that all through the two preceding periods United States superiority over the Soviet Union in the nuclear field was offset, within the framework of global strategy, by Russian superiority in conventional arms and by the Red Army's continued ability to overrun Western Europe either in a matter of days, as during the years from 1946 to 1953, or with more difficulty in the years after 1953.[12] In abstract terms, the balance could be expressed in the following formula: the vulnerability of Soviet territory to United States air strikes was canceled out by vulnerability of the European sector of the Atlantic Alliance, first to invasion and air attack, later to medium-range ballistic missiles (of which several hundred, aimed at targets in Europe, had been installed, as of 1963).

[12] According to the estimates of American intelligence, Russian superiority on the central front in Europe no longer exists.

What happened in the course of these different periods, and what actions or failures to act can one legitimately ascribe to nuclear weapons and to the balance of nuclear power between the United States and the Soviet Union?

If we now look back on the initial phase, 1945 to 1950 (or 1951)—the period of unilateral deterrence when the West was farthest ahead in the atomic field and farthest behind in conventional arms—it is hard not to feel a mixture of surprise and disappointment. It would be most difficult to attribute any major influence on international relations to these weapons. To be sure, there were, and still may be, observers firmly convinced that the Red Army would have occupied all of Western Europe in 1945 or 1946 had it not been for the atom bomb. This hypothesis, though it cannot be conclusively disproved (how can one prove that what did not happen would have happened if one circumstance had been different?), strikes me as extremely unlikely. Soviet cities lay in ruins, the country's economy had to be rebuilt, and Eastern Europe had to be absorbed into the Soviet system. And even if Britain and the United States had actually demobilized their armies—which they might not have done without an atomic monopoly—I still wonder whether Stalin would have risked a third World War on the perilous assumption that, having gone to war to keep Hitler from unifying Europe under Nazi rule, the British and Americans would idly stand by and watch him carry out the *Führer's* grand design.

But even if we discard this unlikely hypothesis, the fact remains that throughout the era of unilateral deterrence it was, as a rule, the Soviet Union that called the signals. On the pretext of technical difficulties the Soviet Union imposed a blockade on West Berlin, which the Americans, instead of dispatching an armed convoy, countered with an airlift. And it was at least with the consent, if not by the order, of the Soviet Union that the North Koreans crossed the 38th Parallel in their attempt to unify Korea by force of arms. All through this period it was as though the Soviet Union decided to make up for its manifest inferiority in atomic arms by an equally manifest aggressive hostility.

This in itself seems to strike some observers as a plausible explanation of what took place: according to them, Russian resentment of humiliating inferiority was sublimated in a display of aggressive belligerency. The greater the external threat, the more determined the effort to counter it by a show of strident self-confidence. Personally, I am not at all convinced by this particular interpretation. During the years that Stalin was really afraid—from 1934 to 1940—he behaved quite differently. I therefore incline to a different psychological explanation of the paradox posed by the aggressiveness of the weaker.

The Bolsheviks in their strategic planning have always given psychological factors a major role. Stalin and the men around him had the greatest respect for American industry and technology; but this respect did not extend to the ability of American leaders to mobilize the immense resources at their disposal in the service of their political objectives. The Russians were never afraid of American atomic weapons simply because they were convinced, quite rightly, that these weapons would never be used against them unless they themselves first resorted to open aggression or extreme provocation.

It is possible that the United States monopoly nevertheless exerted some influence in certain instances. At the time of the Iranian crisis of 1946 it may have been a factor in persuading the Soviet Union to evacuate Northern Iran and leave the Azerbaijan People's Republic, founded under Red Army protection, to its own devices. But essentially the United States confined itself in Europe to a purely defensive use of its atomic monopoly, drawing a line of demarcation and threatening with massive retaliation anyone crossing it in strength and with regular armies. As for the rest of the world, the course of the Chinese civil war and the fringe areas of the cold war generally were not affected by the balance of armed strength. It is difficult in any event to see how the United States could possibly have prevented the Chinese Communists' victory by brandishing its atom bombs. In fact, when North Korean troops crossed the line of demarcation, onlookers as well as participants in both Europe and the United States debated the appropriate response, but none proposed atomic retaliation. Besides, where would the atom bombs—still in short supply at the time—have been dropped? On the cities of North Korea, or on those of the Soviet Union? No North Korean city warranted so monstrous a weapon; furthermore, had it been used a second time by whites against a non-white population, the colored peoples of the entire world would have condemned it as an act of despicable racism. On the other hand, to attack the cities of those who inspired or instigated the aggression would have meant spreading the conflict; this, too, was out of the question.

With the end of the United States' atomic monopoly and unilateral deterrence, speculation about what might have been began: would not the Soviet Union, had it been in the position of the United States, have been able to press its advantage more successfully? Such questions are hard to answer even today. Bertrand Russell at the time urged the United States to threaten the Soviet Union with atomic weapons unless it accepted some sort of agreement along the lines of the Baruch Plan; this would have prevented what is now referred to as the proliferation of these weapons, of which Soviet atomic capacity was the first step. Other observers, looking back somewhat more cautiously, wonder if the same threat could not have accomplished the liberation of Eastern Europe.

It is, and forever will be, impossible to answer such questions. But our experience during subsequent phases should serve to make us somewhat more indulgent toward this reluctance to exploit the atomic monopoly more aggressively during the first postwar years. Offensive use of these weapons seems to run counter to some sort of human reflex. The threat to use them, if intended to maintain the status quo or to block aggression, is acceptable precisely because its sole purpose is to make the other side refrain from action. To confront a major power with a choice between withdrawing its armies or having its cities devastated means, on the other hand, being ready, in turn, either to carry out the threat or else to risk humiliation if the ultimatum goes unheeded. The limitations of nuclear weapons as instruments of diplomacy thus became increasingly obvious during the next phase.

Although unilateral deterrence had given way to direct reciprocal deterrence[13] by 1953 or 1954 (whatever the difference in vulnerability between Soviet and United States territory, the latter was now within range of Soviet strategic bombers), the doctrine proclaimed by John Foster Dulles in 1953 would have been theoretically far better suited to the earlier phase of United States monopoly. It stated, or appeared to state, that in the event of aggression anywhere along the line separating the two power blocs the response would not necessarily be either local or conventional and that, instead, the United States reserved the right to choose the place and the weapons.

This doctrine reflected the bitterness engendered in American public opinion by the Korean War. That war had lasted three years—one year of bloody battles followed by two more of dragged-out negotiations punctuated by sporadic fighting; it had been costly in lives and ended less in victory than in a stalemate. Failure to intervene would, of course, have been costly in other ways, and President Truman's decision, for all the misery and devastation inflicted upon Korea, did serve to bolster confidence in American promises and in the value of alliances with the United States. The fact remained, however, that the most powerful nation in the world had proved unable to achieve a decisive victory over a satellite of the Soviet Union

---

[13] The Soviet Union, holding Western Europe as hostage, also exercised a deterrent action on the United States; but deterrence was not direct so long as the American mainland remained invulnerable.

`aided by the Chinese Army. North Korea did not ac-
complish its objective of unifying the entire country by
force of arms, but the United States in turn failed to
do so. By 1953 American public opinion had come to
regard any war fought in Asia with conventional arms
against extremely underdeveloped countries with their
virtually unlimited human resources as wholly irrational and unacceptable. The lives of American soldiers are far too precious to be risked wholesale by
the United States in ground combat with the soldiers
of China recruited from indefatigable peasant masses.

The doctrine of massive retaliation was never translated into action and never could be. At no time during the presidency of General Eisenhower did the
United States ever contemplate settling a local crisis
in one area by responding in another. Dulles did, however, threaten local use of nuclear arms on several
occasions, and by this time increased availability and
miniaturization of these weapons had facilitated their
restricted use.

It is possible that the threat of recourse to nuclear
arms persuaded the men in the Kremlin to sign the
Korean armistice. But since the Chinese about-face on
the question of prisoners took place after Stalin's
death, their agreement to the armistice may just as
possibly have been inspired by a wish to reduce tension between the two blocs, part of an over-all policy
increasingly evident after the death of the deified
tyrant.

In no crisis since then has the threat of massive retaliation been raised, explicitly or implicitly, although
local use of nuclear weapons has been contemplated.
In the Dienbienphu siege of 1954, intervention by

United States carrier-based aircraft was considered but, other reasons aside, the size of the battlefield made the use of atom bombs unwise. When the King of Iraq and his premier, Nuri Saïd, were assassinated in 1958, the subsequent military intervention, involving the landing of United States paratroopers in Lebanon and British paratroopers in Jordan, assumed an even more clearly symbolic character. These landings, carried out with consent of the legally constituted governments, were largely in the nature of messages addressed to any potential aggressors that the West had both the means and the will to act.

If, finally, in the course of this period there was one trouble spot where atomic arms did prove diplomatically effective, it was probably the Formosa Straits. The mere existence of these arms sufficed to deter the Chinese Communists from mounting a massive attack even against Quemoy and Matsu. Limited operations twice ended in failure; the Chinese Nationalist air force defeated that of the Communists in 1958. It may, of course, be argued that Peking's military setbacks obviated the need for nuclear threats, but it seems to me that these threats continue to be a major factor in the situation. The Russians cannot let their Chinese allies cross the line beyond which the use of nuclear weapons by the United States Seventh Fleet would become at least a possibility, while less provocative measures are inadequate to gain the objective.[14]

But in Europe more than anywhere else the differences between the first and second phases became clearly evident. Between 1946 and 1950 Europe had

[14] At the same time the nuclear threat has contributed to the Moscow-Peking split.

virtually no military forces. The North Atlantic Treaty was signed in 1949, and in 1950, following the Korean crisis, the North Atlantic Treaty Organization (NATO) was established, creating a peacetime integrated military organization comprising the armed forces of all member states of the alliance.

In Europe the Korean aggression gave rise to fear of an all-out war that no one had previously regarded as a serious possibility. Although, in the light of subsequent events, this fear appears unfounded, Korea might after all have been a mere prelude to a broader attack, or else the conflict might have spread without the explicit intent of either side. More carefully reserved was the attitude of certain leaders who felt that the West was deliberately handicapping itself in the cold war as long as Europe was left defenseless, thus constituting a sort of hostage rather than one of the most important stakes in any possible war.

As soon as such a war seemed possible, European leaders, "rushing backward into the future," unearthed the experiences of the preceding one and, with their still green memories of occupation and liberation, loudly proclaimed that they wished to be defended and not liberated this time; only ruins or corpses would be liberated. The NATO constitution for the first time forces statesmen to agree on a strategic doctrine, and one that takes into account both conventional and nuclear arms.

It was this situation that raised the simple and crucial question: what was to be the function of NATO troops? Three answers were logically possible and were given either in turn or simultaneously.

The first envisages NATO forces as a sort of fire-alarm triggering mechanism: they would be able to resist a Soviet advance with enough strength to create the *casus belli atomici,* at which point the Strategic Air Command would take over and unleash an atomic attack.

This answer is open to an immediate objection, for while the Strategic Air Command might conceivably devastate Russia, Europe would still be overrun and occupied. Actually this objection would be valid only on the assumption that deterrence would fail and could have been disregarded at a time when invulnerability of the United States mainland rendered such an assumption very unlikely. But leaders at the time were not too clear about the differences between a strategy of deterrence and a strategy of use following failure of deterrence. Also they more or less expected NATO troops to serve two other functions, perhaps not immediately, but in the not-too-distant future.

First, they were to offset the approximately twenty-five divisions that the Soviet Union continued to keep in East Germany as a permanent invasion threat to West Germany. Even a partial counterweight to this force was bound to bring about changes in the total picture. For one thing, it would prevent Soviet action even on the local level without prior concentration of troops transported from the Soviet Union, a move that would immediately alert the West and thus eliminate the surprise factor essential to any operation aiming at partial conquest with a minimum risk of all-out war.

Second, NATO troops were to counter any aggression on the part of the Soviet Army without recourse to nuclear arms. This desire for an equilibrium at the level of conventional forces was justified by its pro-

ponents in a number of ways; some reiterated their
resolve to be "defended rather than liberated," while
others were anticipating a thermonuclear stalemate,
with Russian capability matching that of the United
States and the American deterrent therefore having
lost all or most of its credibility, for the more vulnerable the American mainland, the less convincing are
United States threats and promises to sacrifice New
York or Boston in order to save Berlin or Paris.

The theory of an arms balance at the conventional
level in its extreme form was apparently envisaged
by NATO councils during an initial phase, but the
goal was to be approached over a period of several
years. The figure of ninety divisions, agreed upon at
Lisbon in 1952, was subsequently reduced to thirty;
this figure of thirty well-armed and well-equipped divisions has since become a sort of fetish and keeps
popping up ritually in speeches delivered on all sorts
of occasions without anyone's really knowing whether
it was ever based on exact calculations in the first
place.

It was this desire for conventional balance of a sort
that first made the Western governments propose rearmament of the German Federal Republic in 1950;
they realized their wish in 1954. And NATO military
leaders, unable to obtain the number of divisions
needed to do the job entrusted to them, received authority to include tactical nuclear weapons in their
planning so that the defense of Western Europe—that
is, the barrier against invasion and occupation—would
not have to rely merely on conventional arms.

So much for the balance sheet of that interim period between unilateral deterrence and the development of ballistic missiles. All through it Europeans were haunted by fear:[15] fear of another enemy occupation, and fear of "American belligerence," or at least of Europe's becoming embroiled in a conflict started elsewhere in the world. Ten years ago Europeans claimed to be afraid that the Americans might be too quick on the trigger; today they fear the opposite. Their shift in attitude is certainly understandable; a war during the earlier phase would have hit Europe far more devastatingly than it would the United States, while the present vulnerability of the United States mainland logically suggests the opposite.

Inside Europe, nuclear weapons have certainly exerted an influence upon relations between the Atlantic allies, since NATO has become the object of their deliberations as well as, sometimes, a bone of contention between them (European Defense Community, German rearmament). In East-West relations, nuclear weapons have tended to favor the status quo between the two blocs, but it is not possible to claim that it would have been upset if these weapons had not been available.

As for the world outside Europe, it does not seem that the existence of nuclear weapons or the balance of nuclear and over-all power between Russia and the United States or their respective blocs had any serious impact upon the disintegration of colonial empires, the crises in the Middle East, and the outcome of the wars in Algeria and Indochina. The failure of the Suez ex-

---

[15] To what extent it was truly deep-felt fear as against a histrionic display is a moot question.

`pedition can scarcely be attributed to the vague threat contained in Marshal Bulganin's letter. Acquisition of thermonuclear arms and of a strategic air force coincided with an upsurge in Soviet diplomatic activity throughout the Middle East, Africa, and Latin America, but this dynamic effort may not necessarily have been the consequence of progress toward thermonuclear equality. The Russians no longer insist that "who is not for us is against us"; uncommitted nations are receiving Soviet economic assistance, and military aid is being extended to countries such as Nasser's Egypt, which persecutes its own local brand of communists. But this increasing flexibility of Soviet diplomacy since the death of Stalin results from a variety of causes, among which nuclear weapons seem to me the least important.

Perhaps the most truly effective, if also the least visible, influence of these weapons is reflected in the extreme caution that the Big Two have exercised in relation to one another,[16] although the Americans have certainly been conspicuously more careful than their rivals. The Hungarian uprising broke out in October–November 1956, at a time when SAC had reached peak strength and the Soviet strategic air force was relatively weak. No intercontinental missile was as yet operative anywhere. United States superiority in a direct confrontation with the Soviet Union would have been crushing, and yet the only assistance the Hungarian revolutionaries received from across

[16] The Berlin blockade was imposed by stages, and prompt United States reaction could probably have averted it. The Korean attack seems to have been a miscalculation; the withdrawal of United States troops had been mistakenly read as proof of American indifference.

the ocean were words of encouragement in the United Nations.

Could the United States have intervened? The Nagy government was recognized as legal, and the Russians were held guilty of aggression in the United Nations. The Americans, without even the threat of all-out war, could have taken at least partial measures, such as moving troops across the demarcation line by way of a warning shot. Events in Hungary, of course, happened to coincide with the Suez Canal crisis, not to mention the presidential elections in the United States; this combination of circumstances certainly helped to paralyze the West, and provided an additional reason for President Eisenhower not to risk dramatic initiatives. But it does not seem likely that, even if the circumstances had been different, the United States would have intervened with force in Hungary, or that Western Europeans would have clamored for it.

Armed conflict with each other has never been the objective of either Russia or the United States.[17] Each has been ready to make or, rather, wanted to make life as difficult as possible for the other; and if they did not display the same measure of belligerence, still each did its best to exploit whatever difficulties the other happened to be having anywhere in the world. But neither side—the stronger because it was unwilling, the weaker because it could not afford to run the risk of all-out war—would attack the other's vital in-

[17] The only instances of direct challenge by the Soviet Union, i.e., crossing the 38th Parallel and sending missiles to Cuba, were effectively countered by the United States. Both, it seems, were the result of mistaken notions in the Kremlin of what Americans are like.

terests as defined by the lines of military demarcation.

In short, two rather familiar principles have dominated diplomatic relations between the Big Two for
the past fifteen years: one, respect for the lines of
demarcation—or, if this seems a more acceptable formulation, opposition to the crossing of these lines by
regular armies (the 38th Parallel being the exception)
—and two, constant challenge of all frontiers and of
all internal governments by political or semiviolent
means. Radio waves and guerrilla forces move freely
across borders that will stop armored vehicles. These
are the two principles of what some call the cold war
and others, peaceful coexistence.

Atomic strategy has been called a failure; yet the
term is deceptive, applicable only where illusions as
to the diplomatic value of nuclear weapons have been
harbored. How could the superiority of SAC or of
tactical atomic weapons have won the struggle against
Vietminh guerrillas or Algerian fellaghas? How could
they have prevented Soviet military aid to Egypt?
How could they have restored to Britain the equivalent of the Army of India, instrument of British power
in the Middle East? Atomic and thermonuclear bombs
did offset the Red Army; and if the West had wanted
to pursue an offensive strategy, it would have had to
outstrip the Soviet Union in conventional arms. There
seems to have been some inclination to do just this in
1950–51, but the effort would have made sense only
if the West had been firmly determined to drive back
Soviet troops, either by force or by threat, and to
liberate the countries that the West refers to as satel-

lites.[18] This was never true. Instead, the West was able to limit its rearmament to a modest scale compatible with economic reconstruction by accepting Soviet superiority in conventional arms. Under these circumstances, nuclear arms could not possibly have contributed any more than they did—that is, equilibrium on the higher level and the safety of the Old World west of the Iron Curtain. This left the nations of Europe with resources needed in a struggle that was being waged on other continents, with different military techniques and different political weapons.

It is conceivable, of course, that the safety of the Old World was never in any danger to begin with, that this danger loomed only in the imagination of the West, and that the Soviets had no intention of marching to the shores of the Atlantic. Still, the idea might have occurred to them in time. One might also argue that it would have been much better if France had not been able to send an expeditionary force to Indochina and a large army to Algeria. But a strategy that affords the commander in the field some freedom of action is not to be blamed for the poor use he makes of his opportunities.

[18] Perhaps also if the West had wanted to obtain complete equality at the level of conventional arms.

2

The Strategic Theory Takes Shape

In the preceding chapter I deliberately refrained from examining the third phase, which began when medium-range and, later, intercontinental ballistic missiles became operative. As of this writing, we are still in the midst of it; and in order to understand the period through which we are living, we need some knowledge not only of weapons and means of delivery but also of the strategic theory that has gradually taken shape in the United States during the past ten years and is now providing guidance for Washington's decisions.

From 1945 to 1955 strategic thinking was in a rather rudimentary state of development, as evidenced by everything from press comments to deliberations at the high executive level. But as the theories elaborated in the research institutes and universities became known in government circles, it evolved rapidly under the pressure of events. Particularly important were the increased vulnerability of the American mainland, resulting in reciprocal rather than unilateral deterrence or, more precisely, deterrence by atomic threat,[1] and the availability of ballistic missiles. In-

---

[1] These formulas are not strictly accurate, since any weapon may under given circumstances become an instrument of deter-

creased United States vulnerability for the first time prompted examination of the various ways in which a conflict between two countries supplied with missiles and thermonuclear warheads might be fought; development of missiles, on the other hand, added the element of *time contraction* to the *space shrinkage* already brought by the strategic air force. In 1914 statesmen still had days for deliberation and negotiation, in the 1940s the speed of bombers reduced that fateful period to mere hours. Ballistic missiles now cut the hours down to minutes.

Strategic theory has never been expounded in quite the form in which it will be sketched here. The small group of what might be called professional theorists are understandably too busy with their work and their differences to bother to formulate the basic ideas held in common by all of them. The account that follows may, therefore, not be accepted by any one of these specialists as an expression of his own personal views.

As long as one side was able to threaten the other without thereby exposing itself to a comparable counterthreat, the problem seemed relatively simple; it amounted to defining the circumstances in which the threat would be translated into action. If the threatened nation remained within the prescribed limits, the threat became at the same time pointless and possibly effective—because the line might have been crossed,

---

rence. The game warden's shotgun deters the poacher. The Red Army was an instrument of deterrence vis-à-vis the United States. "Unilateral deterrence by atomic threat" would be the right way to put it; but "deterrence" has become the accepted term meaning "deterrence by atomic threat," and I have followed this usage for the sake of brevity wherever there is no danger of ambiguity.

after all, if implementation had not been feared. But when the duel is fought between equals, both equipped with missiles and thermonuclear warheads, a great many questions arise.

First, there are the relations between the two deterrent forces; in other words, what happens if one nation strikes first?

This question constitutes the introductory chapter of the theory, so to speak. It involves two distinctions of major significance: one between *first strike* (initiating nuclear attack) and *second strike* (response to it), and another between *counterforce strategy* (the attacker would normally strike at the enemy's means of retaliation) and *countercity* or *countervalue strategy* (if the enemy's reprisal forces are invulnerable, the strike must aim at his vital capacity, his cities). Which of various situations develops depends on whether either or both sides have a strategic counterforce capability, on first or second strike.

These two distinctions permit the resolution of a paradox: for years people have been wondering—and with good reason continue to do so—when or whether the threat of nuclear bombs constitutes an effective deterrent, while giving little thought to the question of what happens if the deterrent fails to deter. Would it really be in the interests of the side using the threat as a deterrent to carry it out if that would involve as much devastation for itself as for the enemy? Such questions force us to realize that strategy and speculation must be pursued beyond the first exploding atom bomb and that other forms of warfare, even of nuclear warfare, are conceivable in addition to what I call *homicidal folly,* described as *nuclear spasm* by American specialists, in which each side simply hurls at the other all the bombs in its possession. This leads to another set of concepts, equally essential: the distinction between the *strategy* (or phase) *of deterrence* by means of the atomic threat, and the *strategy of use* of atomic weapons;[2] in other words *there is a variety of ways in which an atomic war may conceivably be fought.*

The moment we shed the oversimplified and deceptive notion of *the* war, or of the rigidly inflexible choice between limited and all-out war, we automatically re-establish the continuity between traditional and nuclear strategy and, even more, between various methods of deterrence, among which conventional arms loom as large as nuclear ones, even if their functions differ. Maximum security is based on the sum total of arms and their deployment, but the concept of maximum security itself takes on a twofold meaning. While the purpose of the military apparatus is the highest degree of deterrence possible, it must also effectively minimize the risk that, should deterrence fail, escalation will be the only alternative to surrender. In other words, some thought devoted to the strategy of actual use as well as the strategy of deterrence will soon reveal the vast complexity of relations between opponents who, in addition to being enemies, are also linked by a common desire to avoid mutual annihilation.

The quest for deterrence runs parallel to the quest for stability. It would be dangerous to aim at a level

---

[2] The importance of this distinction is illustrated by the earlier remark: it is by no means certain that should deterrence fail, it would be in one's best interest to carry out the threat.

of deterrence that puts the enemy into an intolerable position and thus provokes him into aggressive initiatives. Maximum deterrence does not necessarily coincide with maximum security; if A exerts maximum deterrence against B by virtue of his ability to destroy the overwhelming majority of B's reprisal weapons, B will be tempted in a crisis to jump the gun and get in his blow before the enemy can mount the strike that would disarm him. This would not produce stability, if stability is defined as a situation in which neither side is tempted to strike.

An article by Albert J. Wohlstetter, "The Delicate Balance of Terror," which appeared in the January 1959 issue of *Foreign Affairs,* has played a vitally important role in shaping the strategic theory; its conceptual framework remains valid even though the factual data have since been substantially modified.

Let us begin with an idea simple enough in itself but still too often neglected:[3] there is a fundamental difference between having a few atomic or thermonuclear bombs and a few bombers and possessing a deterrent force. A deterrent force, in fact, does not exist until such time as it is capable of inflicting *reprisals,* and therefore of *surviving attack by an enemy* whom one tried to deter.[4] A reprisal capability of this order

[3] We refer to arguments about the French deterrent and the ability of Mirage IV bombers to breach Soviet defenses; how many distinguish explicitly between a first and second strike?

[4] In certain complex situations a small deterrent may be of some value because the one major power may be reluctant to destroy it for fear of how the other might react. But an *autonomous* deterrent exists only by virtue of its ability to survive an enemy attack.

presupposes six conditions, however, according to Wohlstetter's analysis:

1. The system must be stable and, in peacetime, involve normal management at acceptable cost.

2. It must be able to survive an enemy attack.

3. Civilian leaders and military commanders must be able to make and communicate decisions for action even in the aftermath of a possible enemy attack.

4. If the means of delivery are bombers, they must reach enemy territory with enough fuel left to carry out their mission.

5. The delivery vehicles must be able to penetrate the enemy's active defenses when alerted against attack (i.e., they must be able to deal with fighter planes and ground-to-air missiles).

6. Finally, the reprisals must cause destruction sufficiently extensive to deter the enemy despite the civil defense measures that it may have taken.

Let me briefly illustrate some of these points. A deterrent force can disperse its bombers only within certain limits. These planes, complex and costly, require constant and expert maintenance, and neither crews nor equipment can be scattered over too many bases. Permanent air patrols require a relatively large force because of extensive attrition and the resultant cost. The United States Strategic Air Command has never had more than a small fraction of its planes permanently in the air (a reported maximum of 3 to 4 per cent). An air force consisting of fifty planes may need an alert of only a few minutes[5] in order to take off, provided that each plane has several crews assigned

---

[5] In the United States, the warning period is fifteen minutes. In France and Great Britain it would, of course, be less.

to it; but such a force will not be able to maintain several planes permanently in the air.

The second condition, survival capability, raises difficulties of a different order. By definition it can never be entirely fulfilled—protection adequate against one type of attack may fail against another. It would, of course, be easy to show that no major power will ever be certain of destroying *all* the reprisal weapons of its chief rival; but whichever side attains a high degree of probability of destroying the *majority* of such weapons will at least theoretically be tempted to strike in some circumstances.

In essence, there are three methods now being used to assure survival of retaliatory capability: (1) protection of air fields and missile launching sites; (2) multiplication, dispersal, eventual mobility of land bases; and (3) recourse to delivery vehicles such as atomic submarines that are dispersed as well as mobile and difficult to track at the present stage of technical development.

Unprotected air fields, such as those in France, will obviously be vulnerable not only to attack by medium-range missiles equipped with atomic or thermonuclear warheads but also to conventional bombs. Nor would the launching ramps of medium-range Thor or Jupiter missiles (powered by liquid fuel and requiring seven to eight hours for firing) survive a Soviet attack. Specialists can calculate the number of missiles necessary to obtain any degree of probability of destruction at certain bases over given distances.

Destructive capability has for some ten years now been running a race against survival capability comparable to the earlier contest between shell and armor.

The accuracy of long-range ballistic missiles has turned out to be much greater than expected, but burying these missiles in underground silos made it necessary to increase either the number or the power of the warheads in order to achieve a high probability of destruction (90 per cent and above).

Furthermore, survival capability may prove to be irrelevant if the enemy attack cuts communications between civilian leaders and military commanders and between the latter and the bases, air fields, and missile installations. A supposedly responsible French magazine recently published a dramatic article about the "red phone" allegedly within constant reach of the French chief of state, over which, in case of need, he would order the French deterrent force into action. I confess a marked lack of interest in the circumstances that would motivate such an order, since it would involve the death of most of the people of France; still, it would seem fairly obvious that any major power harboring aggressive designs upon France would start out by destroying the "red phone" and the building in which it is located, along with all its occupants—none of which would seem to present much of a problem. It is also not enough merely to have a few atomic submarines, one of them always at sea; the command post ashore must also be able to survive an attack if anyone is to order the cruising submarine into action.

As the elaborate American efforts indicate, maintenance of these command and communications systems appears to be a task of extraordinary difficulty and complexity, involving both technology and civil engineering. Civilian and military command posts must be protected and ways devised to safeguard radio

communications in an atmosphere modified by thermonuclear explosions.[6]

Let us assume that both these initial obstacles have
been overcome; part of the deterrent has survived and
has been ordered into action. The bombers (or other
delivery vehicles) will have to penetrate defenses
duly alerted, and in this particular area the old struggle between shell and armor is still being waged without any conclusive results: high-altitude bombers are
vulnerable to ground-to-air missiles, and hedgehopping planes to radar or other sorts of missiles. Who
wins in such an encounter? Thus far success has invariably been temporary and relative, temporary because bombers able to penetrate today's defenses may
be helpless against the defenses perfected and installed by 1970; the development of a weapons system
from drawing-board concept to operational readiness
takes at least six years. As of 1963 there probably was
no defense against the Polaris missiles with which nuclear submarines are equipped, but by 1970 the most
important Soviet cities may well be ringed by a network of anti-missile missiles. And success is always
relative because not even a major-power aggressor
can ever be absolutely certain that some vehicles,
even if only a small number, will not survive his attack
and subsequently penetrate his defenses for a retaliatory strike. He can be certain, however, either that
he can destroy the better part of a small enemy force
or that even in the most unfavorable circumstances he

[6] In arguments over the Moscow test ban of August 1963, the
possible effects on communications of multimegaton superbombs
exploded at high altitudes was one of the points raised by
critics.

will sustain only minor damage compared to that which he himself is capable of inflicting.

Any given weapons system has some disadvantages. Nuclear submarines right now represent the least vulnerable element of the deterrent; on the other hand, the warheads of the first Polaris rockets had a power of only 500 kilotons, and the rockets, less accurate than missiles launched from ground installations, were useful only in countercity strategy. Solid-fuel missiles such as the Minuteman can be fired quickly and accurately; they are, moreover, well protected in their silos. But their warheads seem to be only one or two megatons, a relatively weak power that requires correspondingly greater precision if the target is a launching ramp rather than a large city.

I have no wish to reopen here the argument on Wohlstetter's controversial conclusions or to debate whether at the time he wrote the balance of terror was indeed, or was about to become, as precarious as the Rand Corporation study suggested.[7] The article certainly helped to reduce the very dangers it described; the American deterrent was enlarged, diversified, dispersed, hardened. The material data have changed considerably since 1959, but what remains valid for the Big Two as well as for any other country eager to follow them down this road is the theoretical lesson to be learned and the list of problems that still defy ultimate solution because the arms race in our time has become increasingly qualitative rather than quantitative. It is a race run in laboratories whose pace is such that for the first time in history entire weapons

[7] The balance was, in fact, already less precarious by the time the article was published in 1959.

systems, developed at the cost of billions of dollars, are retired without ever having been put to any but purely diplomatic use; or we might say that they are scrapped after having served their purpose, which is precisely to render their military use superfluous.

An interesting confrontation took place when Defense Secretary McNamara and Professor Teller appeared before a United States Senate Subcommittee to plead, respectively, for and against ratification of the Moscow test ban agreement of 1963. The problems in dispute were those just formulated, i.e., the survival capability of the reprisal force including weapons, communications, and command systems. As of August 1963 the Russians, everyone agreed, were ahead in the area of superbombs; they had already exploded a 60-megaton bomb and were believed capable of producing a 100-megaton bomb as well. And though still lacking the missiles to deliver such bombs, they seemed likely to acquire them shortly. The problem was whether this partial superiority effectively upset the balance of deterrence.

The United States Defense Secretary denied that it did. Such bombs, he admitted, could be exploded at high altitudes (somewhere in the neighborhood of 100,000 feet) above cities, with incendiary effects covering vast areas (M. Rougeron's hypothesis), but, Mr. McNamara pointed out, it would seem preferable to distribute delivery of the total strike among a number of less powerful warheads in order to saturate enemy defenses. Moreover, he added, superbombs have certain clear disadvantages, if intended as second-strike weapons, because it is both more difficult and more expensive to assure their surviving an enemy first strike—that is, to harden, camouflage or mobilize the huge missiles required for their delivery.

Next, the Defense Secretary dealt with the use of superbombs in a counterforce strike. He admitted that lack of realistic experience as well as lack of precise knowledge concerning the accuracy of Soviet missiles tends to render all estimates mere approximations; but even under the most pessimistic assumptions a single Soviet superbomb could destroy only somewhat less than two hardened and dispersed Minuteman missiles. The Russians are far from possessing the number of superbombs that would be required to destroy the hundreds of missiles already installed, let alone the 950 planned for 1966.[8] As for command posts, they are specially protected, and substitute command posts have also been planned, some of them air-borne; any Minuteman missile could thus receive launching orders from air-borne command posts.

The third major facet of the problem is the ability to penetrate enemy defenses, chiefly by saturating them with decoys and launching salvos rather than single missiles. The doubtful factor here involves the vulnerability of warheads to blast or radiation set off by high-altitude bursts. The basic penetration capability of United States missiles will, according to the Secretary, persist regardless of Soviet countermeasures, however.

Professor Teller, on the other hand, pointed out that conclusions concerning superbombs were tentative and that some of their advantages may well have escaped United States experts. Moreover, a ban on

---

[8] Demands by the military will probably succeed in increasing this number.

`atmospheric tests would make it impossible to determine the resistance of Minuteman silos to blast except by purely theoretical computations. Third, physicists regard atmospheric tests as necessary for the perfection of a defense against missiles. Dr. Teller reasoned as follows: It is not likely that the Russians will develop a foolproof defense against missiles nor is it probable that by a defense against missiles alone they will be able to prevent the penetration of our retaliatory forces. But if our study of missile defense is inadequate, we shall probably not be in a good position to design the most effective penetration aids for our retaliatory force. Under such conditions, it might be possible for the Russians to shoot down the great majority of our retaliatory missiles. This would be particularly true if a Russian first strike had already substantially weakened our Minuteman sites and other second-strike facilities.

Thus even the most pessimistic witness did not claim that the United States would lose its entire retaliatory capability, even under the most unfavorable circumstances. He said that a first strike could destroy a substantial part of the retaliatory force, and that, in turn, a percentage of the missiles launched in retaliation might be downed by missile defenses, possibly high-altitude bursts of superbombs.

As a layman, I will confine myself to two observations: (1) The qualitative arms race goes on even after the test ban; it cannot be stopped because it is part of the contest between shell and armor, meaning, in contemporary terms, the contest between the power and accuracy of counterforce strategy missiles and the protection of missiles and command posts of the retaliatory force, and between the offensive and defensive uses of thermonuclear technology. (2) Where the Big Two are concerned, the component of uncertainty present in all computations precludes definite stabilization of armaments as well as a state of quiet confidence; but it also makes it highly improbable—barring a Hitler-like chief of state—that either side will take risks whose monstrous enormity the experts will not fail to stress in their reports to the laymen—that is, the statesmen who make the decisions.

Wohlstetter's argument in "The Delicate Balance of Terror" should have done away once and for all with the notions of definitive technological stability and of *quick* equalization between large and small nations (the belief that the latter could acquire within a few years' time and at the cost of a few billion dollars a deterrent or retaliatory force able to command the respect of even the largest of nuclear powers). No such stability or equalization has come about during the past fifteen years, and no such thing is in sight for the next fifteen.

If the preceding analysis has shown that the qualitative arms race is inevitable in this era of advancing science and technology, speculation on the situations that might face two or more nations in possession of nuclear arms may, in like manner, help to enrich and invigorate strategic theory. Without in any way claiming to exhaust all possible contingencies, I shall here examine only duels, i.e., relations between two nations, and for the time being disregard all arms other than nuclear ones and their means of delivery.

Two basic situations of opposite significance derive

`from either opponent's ability or inability, real or imagined, to destroy his adversary's retaliatory capability. If each is able to destroy the other's reprisal force, the situation becomes extremely unstable because whoever strikes first stands to gain everything, while hesitation may mean disaster. This state of affairs corresponds to what I referred to in *Peace and War Among the Nations*[9] as the Case of the Two Gangsters, or the impunity of crime. I am by no means convinced that we are dealing here with a purely theoretical construction with no counterpart in reality: Israel and Egypt, for instance, might well reach precisely this point. Given two countries such as France, each possessing a few dozen nuclear bombs and fighter-bombers, the first to strike is liable to destroy most, if not all, of the enemy's retaliatory force.

At the opposite extreme we have a situation of very great stability, in which the reprisal forces of both sides are invulnerable and neither is superior in counterforce capability. Let us add that both have the power to destroy most of the enemy's large cities, and we get the joint-suicide formula beloved by journalists.

Obviously there is a broad range of intermediate possibilities, between the extreme of *joint suicide* at one pole and *impunity of crime* at the other, apparent the moment the asymmetry, or inequality, of the duelists' respective counterforce and countercity capability is taken into account. Inequality of counterforce action potential involves a twofold risk of instability. If one side, and one side only, has the means to inflict considerable damage upon the enemy's retaliatory

[9] This book, published in 1962, will appear in the United States some time in 1965.

force without thereby being able to wipe it out completely, it will be tempted to strike the moment it suspects the other of harboring actively aggressive designs (utilizing its own counterforce capability to weaken any subsequent blow by the enemy), while the other side, having little or no counterforce capability, will be even more anxious to beat the enemy to the draw, because the vulnerability of its deterrent would leave it completely disarmed in the event of a pre-emptive enemy strike.

In other words, an analysis limited to the duelists and their retaliatory force will make the observer, and to a certain extent even the duelists themselves, prefer symmetry to asymmetry in counterforce capability, at least in situations where even the weaker side still retains a massive first-strike countercity capability and can mount a substantial second-strike attack against cities. At the higher levels of thermonuclear arms, relative superiority may not always be preferable to true equality unless this superiority proves so clearly overwhelming as to deter any and all initiatives on the part of the weaker party.

This sort of stability obviously exerts some influence upon the efficacy of deterrence; one cannot use joint suicide as a constant threat. For even if both duelists actually come to regard the use of thermonuclear weapons as tantamount to suicide, neither can be absolutely sure that the other will not resort to them just the same. Rage has a way of overwhelming the fragile restraints of reason, and there have been Caesars determined to lead their whole nations to death. Barring extreme provocation on its own part or outright madness on the part of its adversary, however, each side would consider recourse to massive counter-city strategy as highly improbable, knowing that it would inevitably call forth reprisals in kind. At the same time, both duelists would certainly come to believe that the thermonuclear threshold had risen considerably.

One of the very early theoretical notions, already accepted in the days of unilateral deterrence, was that of the so-called *atomic threshold*. It meant simply that a border incident or act of local aggression would not be answered by atomizing a city of either the aggressor or his instigator. The significance of this threshold concept, valid since the phase of American monopoly, has become far more evident in the model here under analysis—that is, reciprocal quasi-invulnerability of thermonuclear weapons. As the deterrent forces become progressively less vulnerable, the marginal area within which military operations can be conducted without eliciting thermonuclear responses must inevitably grow larger. In this sense today's more flexible ideas tend to confirm the intuition of those military and civilian leaders who, back in 1951, urged NATO reinforcement in conventional arms because they foresaw a decline in the deterrent effects of nuclear arms threats once the American monopoly had given way to approximate parity between the Big Two.

At this point the analysis becomes considerably more complex, requiring simultaneous attention both to asymmetry at the level of thermonuclear arms and to the disparity of conventional forces. The basic question concerns the precise conditions under which a state that possesses thermonuclear weapons may engage in local operations with conventional arms without having to fear a nuclear response from its rival. The first and most obvious such condition is one in which the opponent lacks the ability decisively to damage the thermonuclear reprisal force of the aggressor. The duelist who, by striking first, can seriously weaken his adversary's retaliatory capability will thereby—according to abstract reasoning—prevent aggressive moves on the part of his opponent, even those conducted with conventional arms. A vulnerable force cannot serve as a "shield." This reasoning, in the eyes of certain American theoreticians, compels the United States to maintain its superiority vis-à-vis the Soviet Union in the form of a strategic first-strike counterforce capability, because such superiority broadens the range of possible moves against which the nuclear threat can act as deterrence.

Assuming that one side has an invulnerable thermonuclear force, will this permit it to use conventional forces as a sword? Even if for the moment we leave aside complications arising out of the reciprocal relationship of the conventional forces, it is obvious that the protection afforded by the so-called thermonuclear shield will not inspire much confidence if the opponent possesses a massive first-strike countercity capability. In theory, at least, a country unable to absorb the enemy's retaliatory blow *ought not* to be the first to resort to nuclear arms unless its very life is at stake. But if such a country were able to destroy *only half of its enemy's cities* on a first strike, it would still arouse considerable fear even in an adversary supplied with an invulnerable retaliatory force that in turn would wipe out *all the cities* of the aggressor. In short, while `invulnerability of the thermonuclear "shield" is a prerequisite to the use of conventional forces as a "sword," it is not sufficient in itself. A further requirement is weakness of the enemy's strategic first-strike counter-city capability; moreover, the side wanting to wield the conventional "sword" must not have cause to fear its rival's outright madness.

American analysts have barely touched upon the conditions under which a nation might avail itself of its "conventional sword" in order to advance under the protection of the "thermonuclear shield." On the other hand, they have dwelt extensively upon conditions under which, despite growing invulnerability of the thermonuclear systems, the United States may be able to maintain the efficacy of its deterrent for the benefit of those of its allies located at the perimeter of the Eurasian land mass, within the immediate vicinity of the potential aggressor.

At the level of rarefied abstraction on which this analysis unfolds, they have come up with three answers to the problem. The first is to maintain a strategic counterforce capability. As long as the United States can inflict extensive damage upon the retaliatory weapons of a potential aggressor, the latter *rationally ought not* to initiate extreme provocation or make full use of his superiority in conventional arms. A second answer is to increase the production of conventional arms; a potential aggressor can exploit the reciprocal paralysis of thermonuclear systems only if his superiority is sufficiently overwhelming to guarantee him swift and certain seizure of his objectives. In this sense conventional arms still constitute a deterrent as they have throughout history, but with more chance of success because in the background there always looms the danger of escalation to the use of the ultimate weapons. The third and last solution is to substitute a graduated (or flexible) response for an all-out one.[10]

This last concept occupies a central position in the American theory and accounts for the major part of the European dissension. Let us imagine two thermonuclear systems, both progressively more invulnerable, and one side possessing conventional forces with decisive superiority, at least at the local level. In such a situation the best strategy would aim to avoid being trapped in the either-or alternative of apocalypse versus surrender—inevitable if the aggressor is immediately threatened with total response involving all the weapons of massive retaliation—and, on the contrary, to plan for graduated responses so that the use of neither conventional nor tactical atomic weapons, nor even of the first missiles, would have to lead inexorably to the use of the ultimate weapons. In its initial phases the strategy of use would still constitute part of a warning addressed to the enemy in the hope of convincing him that there would be no surrender and that he, too, had a stake in coming to terms.

Such a strategy of use obviously requires a thermonuclear system that is at the same time powerful and relatively invulnerable. The greater its vulnerability, the narrower the range of possibilities between the absence of hostilities on the one hand and all-out war on the other. No analyst, of course, can ever be sure that the actual course of events will follow his scenario

[10] In addition to these specifically military responses there are the psychological ones, with which we shall deal further on. See p. 201 and ff.

and that the duelists will pursue their hostile moves
into the initial phases of nuclear exchanges without
going on to extremes. For the moment, however, we
are concerned not so much with the probability of
realizing these abstract schemes as with understanding
the logic behind the strategic concept.

This logic happens to be simple and compelling, in
the hypothesis as postulated. Lacking parity in conventional arms, a duelist could not and should not
give up the threat of possible escalation, but neither
should he adopt a military stance in which inadvertent
or limited hostilities would automatically touch off
escalation all the way to the highest level. These two
conditions can be met and reconciled only by a strategy involving the controlled use of nuclear weapons,
which presupposes a fairly well-protected thermonuclear apparatus and plans sufficiently diversified so
that, even after the crisis has become acute and the
lower levels have been passed, the choice still is not
limited to the alternatives of defeat versus thermonuclear spasm.

The strategy of progressive and rational use of
atomic and thermonuclear weapons would seem to
demand equally strong nerves on the part of both
duelists, a comparable invulnerability of their thermonuclear systems, and a similar diversification of their
operational plans. There has been no shortage of critics
to stress the wide gap that separates such speculations from actual experience and to point out the unpredictability of events. I shall confine myself to two
general observations: the less invulnerable and the
less capable of differentiated action the deterrent
force, the greater the risk of escalation in any clash

between duelists at any stage of the acute crisis. And the side that neglects to prepare such a strategy ahead of time might nonetheless be led to practice it under certain conditions.

On the other hand, it seems perfectly obvious that a strategy involving the graduated use of atomic weapons is wholly beyond the ability of nations possessing a numerically small and poorly protected deterrent, good only for countercity strategy when directed against a major power.[11] This explains the scornful animosity with which American proponents of the graduated response have regarded the notion of small national deterrents. Within the Atlantic Alliance such deterrents are pointless because the American system, even in its second-strike capability, is sufficiently powerful to destroy the majority of Soviet cities. If, the argument continues, the small forces are intended rather as purely national, they again serve no useful purpose during the phase of deterrence—from what conceivable move that American power is unable to stop could they deter the Soviets?—while in the phase of possible use they are liable to become downright dangerous by interfering with the rational conduct of operations.

The theory whose conceptual framework I am here attempting to outline has been worked out by American analysts on the basis of the world situation as well as the position of the United States itself. Moreover, two key ideas that justify and give direction to these

[11] If this small force were facing another of like size it might conceivably have some strategic counterforce capability. But the instability of reciprocal strategic counterforce capability would make matters even worse.

`considerations remain valid despite the fact that in Europe they evoke reactions ranging from polite skepticism to outright hostility.

The first is that there are degrees even of horror. The difference between being able to drop a few atom bombs on enemy cities and annihilating a nation is greater, not smaller, than the difference between the military potential of big and small powers used to be in the past. It is conceivable that beyond a certain point these disparities in destructive potential eventually level off; but that would be a psychological assumption rather than a theoretical truth. At the moment of crisis such disparities as exist in strategic counterforce or countercity capability, and in first-strike or second-strike capability, between Russia and the United States, may not exert any influence whatsoever. This proposition is not self-evident and can be neither proved nor disproved; but in any event such reasoning, relevant to relations between the Big Two, for the time being applies to them alone.

The second idea is that thermonuclear war, though not desired by either of the present duelists, may break out just the same. Few theoreticians regard this contingency as probable within the next twenty years,[12] but all of them maintain—and I do not see how one could deny this—that it would be unreasonable constantly to brandish the threat of nuclear retaliation and at the same time to assume it would never be necessary to carry it out. The war for which one prepares so as not to have to fight it, though sometimes

---

[12] I know of one who privately told me that he regarded the probability of a major war within the next twenty years as better than one in two.

called "*impossible*," is *possible* just the same. If it were indeed physically or morally impossible, deterrence would cease to operate.

The present improbability of thermonuclear war derives not only from the monstrous horror of these weapons and the fear they inspire—an additional reason is the nature of the conflict between the United States and the Soviet Union. Neither territory nor resources is at stake; each has ample space as well as growth reserves, both extensive and intensive. Their conflict arises from the geometry of international relations—two big powers within one international system, unless they can rule jointly, are bound to be enemies by virtue of their position—and from incompatibility of their respective governments and ideologies. But neither is in a crusading mood or infected with madness to the point where it would lightly resort to thermonuclear arms in order to attain its goals. Socialist or capitalist, Soviet or American, the chiefs of state prefer peaceful coexistence to a thermonuclear war in which their two countries would be the first victims and in which China would stand to gain the most.

The American analysts, while regarding thermonuclear war as possible, have given little thought to conditions under which such a war would *intentionally* be unleashed. They have examined various sets of circumstances that might lead to war without its being deliberately wanted by either of the principals, but they have always assumed a common interest on the part of both Russia and the United States to avoid fighting a war unto death—though sometimes they may have wondered just how acutely Khrushchev, in turn, was aware of it.

In order to include the entire range of possibilities, let us begin with *intentional war* between the United States and Russia—the least likely contingency and one that has received little attention. Let us assume a confrontation between a large nation and a small one. The first has the means completely to destroy the small nation's means of delivery. The small nation is ruled by an unstable regime and an irresponsible leader; the large nation refuses to tolerate the threat of atomic war from an unreasonable man. In such circumstances the most economical and the least inhuman method would be an ultimatum demanding that the small country dismantle its deterrent which, if used for a first strike, could inflict some degree of damage, so that the ultimatum unaccompanied by a warning shot does involve some risk. Every reader is free to imagine what would happen.

This hypothesis seems farfetched, and yet the Cuban episode might well have led to just such an impasse. At the height of the crisis Khrushchev, under the pretext of reassuring Kennedy, wrote to him somewhat along the lines of "don't get excited, these missiles have not been turned over to Fidel Castro but continue to be serviced by Soviet soldiers taking orders only from the Soviet Government." Khrushchev himself thus implied that Kennedy would have had more grounds for worry and action if the Cuban Government *had acquired control* of these missiles.[13]

This historical reminder should suffice to demonstrate that recourse to threat, and even recourse to the

[13] In May 1964 the departure of Russian technicians from Cuba stirred some anxiety in Washington about whether Fidel Castro would use the anti-aircraft missiles against the U-2s.

use of nuclear weapons in order to prevent a country regarded as irresponsible from acquiring such arms, is at least conceivable. I think it very doubtful that the major powers would stand by idly and allow several minor ones to play with nuclear firearms. Under normal circumstances they should be able to impose their will without having to go so far as actually using these weapons, which it is their intention, or illusory hope, never to employ other than rationally—that is, as instruments of diplomacy. But resistance on one side and brutality on the other might well cause fireworks in the end.

Another hypothesis, unfortunately far more probable, would be an intentional war resulting from a duel between two powers either or both of which have vulnerable nuclear forces. Undoubtedly this sort of duel would be a local affair fought between small nations always subject to the risk of intervention and punishment by big ones; but hatred, the passionate determination to kill the enemy to the last man, coupled with the knowledge that the enemy is reciprocating feeling and intent, might precipitate such a situation. This is an abstract conjecture, but it is uncomfortably possible to imagine a real conflict in which both parties might be thus tempted to take the initiative and in which one of them might in fact do so.

An intentional war between the present Big Two has become supremely unlikely. But in order not to slight any hypothesis, however improbable, I might mention a technological breakthrough that would give one of them a clear-cut superiority over the other. One cannot entirely rule out the possibility that if the stakes were high enough—world domination—the power in question might find it difficult to resist temptation and might try to exploit to the limit this favorable if temporary state of affairs. Without actually wanting to start the cataclysm, it might press its advantage so vigorously that it would set it off just the same.

Let us now take a hypothesis far more probable, especially in a period of thermonuclear duopoly. Neither duelist wants a war that would devastate both countries; in what circumstances could it break out just the same, in spite of all their precautions?

The first possibility is *war by accident*. Perhaps the word "accident" should be used in the plural, because various types of accident are conceivable. A bomb may explode as the result of a technological mishap, and the explosion may be misintepreted by the enemy as the start of hostilities. Other accidents would include the misreading of radar blips—such as mistaking a flight of migratory birds for plane formations, a possibility brought up by Gromyko in a United Nations address—or insanity on the part of an officer in a position to issue orders that would set off the fatal chain of events. Science fiction has popularized some rather foolish notions on this score; the mental breakdown of a single individual is not enough to lead all mankind into homicidal madness. Bombers that take to the air in case of an alert, including those headed for designated targets, will return to their bases unless they receive explicit confirmation of the orders to strike. The *fail-safe* (the title of a well-known and execrable book) procedures reduce the probability of such accidents to a minimum, and installation of a direct telephone line between the Kremlin and the White House eliminates the danger of war due to accident about as effectively as such danger can ever be banished from human affairs.

War due to misunderstanding is a vague term covering a multitude of contingencies, all of them improbable but conceivable. The simplest form of misunderstanding, especially in a period when all-or-nothing alternatives dominate strategic thinking, is the failure of deterrence. Thus American leaders might vainly seek to convince their Soviet opposites that any attempt to cut communications between West Germany and West Berlin would be answered by force. If the Soviets misjudge American determination and they or the East Germans shoot down some United States planes, it might mean the start of hostilities that could lead to almost anything.

This example actually illustrates both *war due to misunderstanding* and *war by escalation*. If the response to aggression had been massive retaliation, as it would have been a few years ago, the example would belong to the pure *war due to misunderstanding* type; but now that the West[14] has adopted the theory of graduated response, thermonuclear war presupposes escalation as well as an original misunderstanding. The earlier and unmixed version could now come about only if the country trying to deter had prepared no response other than massive retaliation in the event the aggressor state refused to take the threats seriously and be deterred.

In a *war by escalation* local hostilities initially fought with conventional arms gradually lead to extremes of violence. Fear of precisely this possibility has made

[14] But not the Soviet Union.

both contemporary duelists wary of local operations, and this fact in turn has riddled the whole idea of escalation with paradoxes and contradictions. If the enemies could be absolutely sure that a limited conflict would not spread beyond certain boundaries, they might be less reluctant to press advantages which either side possesses in varying degrees and different localities. So long as there is no complete parity everywhere in the world and at every level of armament, the threat or at least the implied risk of escalation will tend to deter aggression. And yet this legitimate concern about escalation, however justifiable as against the far greater risk of all-out war, will under certain conditions reduce the efficacy of deterrence in regard to minor acts of aggression. Here we have the first example—there will be others—of the antinomies of deterrence; measures taken to meet one kind of danger may themselves tend to increase dangers of a different kind.

The method theoretically best suited to counter the risk of *war due to misunderstanding* is the same as that applicable to *war by accident*—communications between the enemies must be maintained at all times, but most particularly at a time of crisis. Notifying the other party ahead of time in vague terms that "one will not tolerate" this or that is far from enough to prevent misunderstandings. In the Berlin crisis of 1961–62 President Kennedy and Dean Rusk transmitted futile messages of precisely this sort to Premier Khrushchev and Gromyko. The Russians were under no obligation to let themselves be convinced and were, on the contrary, rather duty-bound *not* to accept such statements at face value. Deterrence by its very nature involves an element of bluff, and in nuclear strategy, as in poker, the meaning of messages remains equivocal up to the very last moment—which is precisely why the analysts insist that there must never be "a very last moment" comparable to the declaration of war in ages past; that is, a moment signifying the end of the dialogue and the onset of unlimited violence. No matter how slight the chance of avoiding escalation to extremes once hostilities have started, for the sake of his own country as well as mankind a chief of state must not throw it away; he must continue the dialogue even in the midst of violence. Once again the "hot line" is the symbol of this doctrine, a new formulation of Clausewitz' concept of the inextricable link between strategy and diplomacy.

The methods designed to cope with the risks of *accident* and *misunderstanding* also apply to escalation; but here an additional problem involves differentiating between various types of conflict and various types of weapons. Can limited war be clearly divided from all-out war? A facile answer given by those caught in the trap of fallacious reasoning is that all such attempts at differentiation are bound to fail now that a continuity in explosive power between conventional and thermonuclear arms has been re-established. This type of logic would make escalation almost inevitable; whether or not it took place would depend entirely on circumstantial factors such as area, objectives, character of the antagonists. American analysts, however, tend to view the problem quite differently.

Even if the small tactical atomic weapons are less powerful than the biggest conventional ones, it does not mean that the conscience of the community and of the statesmen in charge no longer makes a distinction between chemical and nuclear explosives. The latter, because of their novelty and immense destructive power, still retain an element of mystery and of horror. They have become the object of a sort of taboo; and government leaders, duty-bound to resist but unwilling to carry hostilities to extremes, will spontaneously refer back to the difference between conventional and nuclear arms as a simple and so to speak symbolic distinction. To abstain from the use of nuclear arms is in itself a message of intent addressed to the enemy-partner who in turn will not fail to grasp its import, especially since no other distinction is likely to suggest itself with equal force to both sides. And an implicit agreement requires just such symbols meaningful to all concerned, a universal language. Enemies no longer overtly communicating with each other need precisely this type of language in order to avoid misjudging each other's intentions. The mere fact that one combatant initially refrains from using nuclear weapons does not, of course, guarantee equal restraint on the part of his enemy; but, at the very least, notice has been served that one side does not want to cross the threshold of the irrevocable.

American specialists did not reach this conclusion immediately nor, for that matter, do they all concur in it. During the preceding phase, when the United States had already lost the atomic monopoly but was still ahead in the duel with the Soviet Union,[15] certain theoreticians, the best-known of whom was Henry A. Kissinger, saw tactical nuclear arms as a means of

[15] In the duel between the Big Two, that is, though not necessarily in the struggle between the two power blocs.

regaining the United States lead. Furthermore, in re-
evaluating the course of international relations during
the years of United States monopoly, they felt that the
United States had failed—either through lack of ability
or through lack of knowledge—to make full use of its
military strength for purposes of diplomacy; they
therefore were casting about for weapons that, in contrast to the strategic arms rendered useless by their
own monstrosity, would again provide eloquent arguments as well as tools in the service of diplomacy, as
armaments had done in earlier historical periods. Tactical nuclear weapons resemble tanks and guns in that
they can be used on the battlefield; they would, moreover, tend to favor the side industrially more developed and technologically more advanced.

A few years later Mr. Kissinger reversed his position.[16] No one, he said, could foresee accurately what
ground warfare with tactical nuclear weapons would
be like. Each of the three branches of service (Army,
Navy, Air Force) assigns different functions to these
weapons, and nothing proves that their use would help
the West. Ever since, the argument of the dissenting
school of thought—that escalation to extremes is made
not inevitable but *more probable* by crossing the
atomic threshold—has fully come into its own.

In addition to *accident, misunderstanding,* and *escalation,* a fourth concept should be listed because it
constitutes one of the targets of United States diplomacy—*irrationality.* The entire American theory is

[16] I am by no means criticizing him for changing his mind;
quite the opposite. For the past ten or fifteen years the theoreticians have been thinking out loud and quite legitimately reach
different conclusions as their thinking changes and new developments occur in weapons and means of delivery.

based on rationality; it attempts to reconstruct the manner in which a strategist would behave if, like his hypothetical counterpart in economic theory, he were both intelligent and well-informed. But how many real-life chiefs of state resemble this idealized portrait? How many of them are always able to abide by the dictates of reason, at least reason defined by the theoreticians?

In any case, the risk of irrational decisions increases with the number of countries acquiring nuclear arms. This increase derives from two separate factors; for one thing, even if we assume that all future participants in the apocalyptic poker game will be as coolly rational as the present two players, the game itself will have become far more complex and less predictable—hence more dangerous. Situations of extreme instability, due to the vulnerability of deterrent forces, may develop locally. Furthermore, countries in possession of nuclear weapons may be at the mercy of military juntas, revolutionaries, or adventurers, and once a truly irresponsible head of government joins in the game, the worst may come to pass.

The worst, may we add, not only for him but for the other players as well. It is easy to imagine how, by the use of even relatively insignificant nuclear forces, he could provoke a chain reaction. The country victimized by his bombs may, for instance, mistake their point of origin—the small nation—and automatically turn on its own rival. Personally I believe that the big powers will act jointly to restrain potential troublemakers, even those armed with nuclear weapons, but the concept of a *catalytic war*—i.e., all-out war provoked by a third (or fourth) country, either deliberately or through clumsiness—keeps haunting the minds of some theoreticians.

This obsession with the *Nth country*, the nation that by manufacturing its own nuclear weapons would upset the present rules of the game by putting an end to the thermonuclear duopoly, explains the dogmatic opposition—almost unanimously shared by all United States analysts—to the spread of nuclear arms. It is a point of view easy for Americans to defend, since their country happens to own the best-stocked arsenal in the world, and rather difficult to assail, since the long-range dangers of nuclear proliferation are self-evident.

American theorists, however, might have given somewhat more thought to nations that, while not underestimating the risks inherent in proliferation, do not themselves possess nuclear arms and hence quite legitimately fear either for their safety or for their autonomy.

Is it possible to distinguish schools of thought among American specialists? In general their opinions differ on three major points.

The majority of the scientists tend to regard the unlimited arms race and the quest for ever more efficient weapons and means of delivery as dangerous and insane. Such competitive bidding would, in their opinion, gain neither side any decisive advantage, while polluting the atmosphere, aggravating international tensions, and magnifying the very danger it is supposed to avoid. Arrayed against this majority of physicists, who hope, if not for disarmament, at least for a slowing down of the qualitative arms race as a first step toward arms control, is a minority, the best known of whom is Dr. Edward Teller. For a variety of reasons—fear of a Soviet technological breakthrough, belief in the fundamentally irreconcilable nature of the political struggle between the Big Two, desire to maintain a margin of United States superiority—this group mistrusts any measures, including partial suspension of nuclear tests, that would tend toward crystallization of parity between Russia and the United States.

This opposition from within the scientific community has found support in the smaller circle of strategic analysts. Which model is to represent the strategic objective of the United States—stability at the upper level of thermonuclear arms, or a certain strategic counterforce capability? Supposing this capability becomes unobtainable, what reinforcements in conventional arms will be required? What role should be assigned to civilian defense?

Finally, another opposition trend concerns relations with the allies of the United States. The majority of analysts, especially those who came to strategy from the natural sciences, are passionately eager to maintain, if not an American monopoly on nuclear arms, then at least unity of operational command. Arms control and safeguarding communications with the enemy seem far more important to them than the susceptibilities of their European allies. Other analysts, fewer in number and trained in political science, such as Henry A. Kissinger, Bernard Brodie, and the team of R. Strausz-Hupé, while not wholeheartedly in favor of a French nuclear force, are more understanding of the French position and more inclined toward either a European deterrent or some compromise with French ambitions for autonomy.

Thus far the dominant influence in Secretary Mc-Namara's circle has been exerted by the scientists, eager above all to slow the arms race and to prevent the spread of nuclear weapons. The assassination of President Kennedy brought about no change on this point. Perhaps President Johnson is even less interested than was his predecessor in reaching an agreement with General de Gaulle, whose recognition of Red China and proposal for Vietnam's neutralization have been interpreted in Washington as the expressions of an anti-American policy.

3

Europe and the McNamara Doctrine

The team of advisers around President Kennedy
and Defense Secretary McNamara included a number
of college professors profoundly influenced by the theoretical speculations outlined in the preceding chapter. McGeorge Bundy was Dean of the Harvard Fac-
ulty of Arts and Sciences before becoming Secretary
to the National Security Council and President Kennedy's special adviser on problems of national security.
Jerome B. Wiesner, presidential science adviser, was
professor at M.I.T. Both men participated in the semi-
nar on arms control that met regularly during the win-
ter of 1960–61. Several of Secretary McNamara's assistants (H. S. Rowen, A. C. Enthoven, C. J. Hitch)
also came from Cambridge and the Rand Corporation.
The Defense Secretary himself had no special background in the economic and strategic problems affecting his new job, but he has tended to rely for advice
on civilian theoreticians rather than military profes-
sionals.

The theses that most of these theoreticians hold in
common were outlined in the preceding chapter; they
will now be re-examined more closely in inverse order.

The world of today is dangerous. The world of to-

morrow, in which some ten or fifteen countries will
have nuclear arms, is bound to be incomparably more
dangerous. The dread of such nuclear proliferation
accounts for the stubborn efforts made by President
Kennedy to reach a *nuclear test ban agreement with
the Soviet Union* as well as for his *opposition to
France's establishment of a national deterrent.*

War may come about through either midunderstand-
ing or escalation; it therefore becomes imperative on
the one hand to maintain constant communications
with the enemy under all circumstances (the "hot
line") and, on the other, to acquire conventional arms
in sufficient quantities so that tactical nuclear weapons
will not have to be used immediately and regardless
of the particular situation, with the consequent risk of
escalation (hence the concepts of *option* and *of pause*).

Precautions against misunderstanding and escalation
in turn require *scuttling the doctrine of massive retaliation* and replacing it by the *doctrine of graduated
response*. A misunderstanding is bound to occur sooner
or later if preparation for any failure of deterrence is
confined to an all-out massive strike. The danger of a
war that no one really wants to fight can be reduced to
a minimum only if the oversimplified and lethal all-or-
nothing concept is buried once and for all. The spirit of
reasoned intent that informs policy must not be allowed
to evaporate the moment the first bombs start exploding; intelligent national policy must to the very end
make a determined effort simultaneously to *safeguard
the national interest* and to *prevent escalation to the
extremes of violence.*

Besides, the measures suggested to minimize the
risk of thermonuclear war in no way conflict with those

indicated for the *reinforcement of deterrence*. In fact, the less vulnerable the deterrent, the more destructively it will retaliate against anyone risking a first strike, so that threats against it will progressively lose *credibility*, or psychological plausibility. A nation that has at its disposal a wide range of possible responses, rather than a narrow choice between thermonuclear apocalypse and capitulation, is far more likely to inspire caution and respect in potential aggressors, including one contemplating more local operations. In other words, an increase in conventional arms and the ability to conduct combat operations without having to resort to nuclear weapons should also be regarded as deterrents, indeed as the means of deterring local aggression against which the threat of massive retaliation might prove futile.

The doctrine of graduated response involves not only raising the nuclear threshold and widening the area of conventional warfare but also, in the version presented by Secretary McNamara, a strategic counterforce phase even as part of the second strike and preceding the total disaster of countercity strategy. To anyone conversant with the evolution of strategic theory as reflected in the literature and the work done at various institutes and universities, nothing is more comprehensible than the concept now referred to as the McNamara doctrine.

Unfortunately most Europeans, including statesmen, politicians, generals and journalists, knew little if anything about the theoretical spadework done before the assumption of leadership by the Kennedy Administration. Unable to grasp the methods of reasoning that had led up to the conclusions then presented with such apparent abruptness, they questioned the strategic counterforce capability that United States spokesmen suddenly claimed for their thermonuclear apparatus a mere few months after they had publicized the missile gap. Without giving much thought to the matter, they assumed that when it came to a deterrent strategy, a graduated response was less effective than a total one—which, to say the least, is far from self-evident. Economic reasons made Europeans spontaneously hostile to any increase in conventional armaments, and they suspected the so-called new doctrine of being a first step toward the *disatomization* of Europe—i.e., a subtle attempt to reduce the risk of involving the American mainland in nuclear devastation while exposing Europe to the destruction involved in a so-called conventional war.

Before discussing the arguments for and against the McNamara doctrine, let us look at the relevant data as given by Mr. McNamara in a statement before the House Armed Services Committee.

The composition of the United States' strategic thermonuclear force as of January 1963 was as follows:[1] 126 Atlas Intercontinental Ballistic Missiles, 54 Titans and 30 Minutemen;[2] in addition, 144 Polaris rockets distributed by clusters of 16 in 9 nuclear submarines. The United States maintains 650 bombers on permanent alert, ready to take to the air within fifteen

[1] According to United States sources, the Soviets at the beginning of 1963 had only 50 to 100 ICBMs.

[2] The Minuteman, now being mass-produced, is coming off the line at the rate of about one a day. Buried in silos, these solid-fuel missiles can be launched quickly and will form the bulk of the deterrent, usable in counterforce strategy.

minutes; this apparently is somewhat less than half the total strength of the Strategic Air Command.

These figures apply only to the Strategic Air Command; fighters or fighter-bombers and light or carrier-based bombers carrying either atomic or thermonuclear bombs constitute a substantial addition to the strategic deterrent. In his testimony, Secretary McNamara stressed that while the strategic deterrent represented the essence of United States retaliatory capability, the tactical forces were coordinated with it, particularly in regard to selection of targets.

Development of the strategic deterrent will have its effects on the missile program. For the time being, Mr. McNamara intends to keep the fourteen B-52 squadrons as well as the two squadrons of supersonic long-range B-58s. The 1963 Minuteman program was increased to 800, with an additional 150 planned for the 1963–64 budget. The nuclear submarine program calls for 41 of these vessels to be constructed; each will carry 16 missiles.

Referring to one of the most contoversial aspects of the American doctrine, the strategic counterforce capability, the Secretary had this to say:

"As the Soviet Union hardens and disperses its ICBM force and acquires a significant number of missile-launching submarines (as we must assume that they will do in the period under discussion [up to 1968]) our problem will be further complicated. . . . Thus, it is even more important today than it was last year that we concentrate our efforts on the kind of strategic offensive forces which will be able to ride out an all-out attack by nuclear-armed ICBMs or submarine-launched missiles in sufficient strength to strike back decisively.

"A very large increase in the number of fully hard Soviet ICBMs and nuclear-powered ballistic missile-launching submarines would considerably detract from our ability to destroy completely the Soviet strategic nuclear forces. It would become increasingly difficult, regardless of the form of the attack, to destroy a sufficiently large proportion of the Soviet's strategic nuclear forces to preclude major damage to the United States, regardless of how large or what kind of strategic forces we build. Even if we were to double and triple our forces we would not be able to destroy quickly all or almost all of the hardened ICBM sites. And even if we could do that, we know no way to destroy the enemy missile-launching submarines at the same time. We do not anticipate that either the United States or the Soviet Union will acquire that capability in the foreseeable future. Moreover, to minimize damage to the United States, such a force would also have to be accompanied by an extensive missile defense system and a much more elaborate civil defense program than has thus far been contemplated. Even then we could not preclude casualties counted in the tens of millions."

This testimony, somewhat more cautious, perhaps, than previous statements, constitutes an explicit admission as to the limits of efficacy that no counterforce strategy can possibly transcend; and those who, by stressing these limits, claim to be refuting the Defense Secretary, are either deluding themselves or their readers.

Following this decisive paragraph, Mr. McNamara came back to one *temporary fact* and one *idea of last-*

ing value. The fact was the strategic counterforce capability that the United States *believes* it has *for the moment:* "We have provided, throughout the period under consideration, a capability to destroy virtually all of the 'soft' and 'semi-hard' military targets in the Soviet Union and a large number of their fully hardened missile sites, with an additional capability in the form of a protected force to be employed or held in reserve for use against urban and industrial areas."[3] The idea of lasting value he expressed as follows: "In talking about global nuclear war, the Soviet leaders always say that they would strike at the entire complex of our military power including government and production centers, meaning our cities. If they were to do so, we would, of course, have no alternative but to retaliate in kind. But we have no way of knowing whether they would actually do so. It would certainly be in their interest as well as ours to try to limit the terrible consequences of a nuclear exchange."

[3] Regarding the number of hard Soviet sites that United States thermonuclear power would be able to destroy, Mr. McNamara said: "This number will not constitute a very large proportion of fully hardened sites, assuming the Soviets construct them." He added: "It takes a lot of missiles to destroy a fully hardened site." How many does it take? The figures are not given. The three factors essential to the computation are circular error probability (c.e.p.), depending on range of shot and guidance of missiles, added pressure which the silos are able to withstand, and the explosive power of the warheads. It is obvious that destruction may be accomplished by fewer missiles if, given increased power, the average c.e.p. remains constant. How many Minutemen does it take to destroy a Soviet silo? Apparently at least half a dozen, possibly more. In August 1963 Mr. McNamara conceded that a 100-megaton warhead would destroy on the average somewhat less than two hard and dispersed missile silos. What we have here is a new chapter in the struggle between shell and armor—i.e., ever more powerful warheads against increased protection.

In other words, the concept of a separate phase of counterforce strategy, preceding the countercity strategy of an all-out war, does not rest on the illusion that the United States would be able to wipe out the entire Soviet retaliatory capability. Rather the concept was introduced, in the resolute hope of preserving up to the very end whatever chances reason and mankind may still have, of acknowledging differences in degree even of nuclear exchanges, and of never unleashing the full fury of homicidal madness before being forced to do so.

Concerning another controversial aspect of the McNamara doctrine, the increase in conventional arms, the Secretary in no way ruled out the use of tactical nuclear weapons by NATO in the event of a massive Soviet attack in Europe, even if the aggressor initially limited himself to conventional arms. Thus it is inaccurate to accuse him of giving the aggressor a choice of arms while denying this same choice to NATO. At least in his testimony before the House Committee, the Secretary merely remarked that "we may well be faced with situations in Europe where it would not be to the advantage of ourselves or our Allies to use even tactical nuclear weapons initially—provided we had the capability to deal with them through nonnuclear means. Nuclear weapons, even in the lower kiloton ranges, are extremely destructive devices and hardly the preferred weapons [rather an understatement, it would seem] to defend such heavily populated areas as Europe."

Nor did Mr. McNamara claim that the use of tactical nuclear weapons would *necessarily* lead to escalation. In a striking phrase he noted that "while it does not necessarily follow that the use of tactical nuclear weapons must inevitably escalate into global nuclear war, it does present a very definite threshold, beyond which we enter a vast unknown." Nothing in this statement justifies suspecting the United States of sinister intentions to withdraw from Europe all tactical nuclear arms (of which there are today at least fifty per cent more than in 1961, when the Kennedy Administration took over).

It is true that the new doctrine, rightly or wrongly, does not admit of the immediate *and* automatic use of atomic tactical weapons. These should be available in case of an all-out attack with conventional weapons that could not otherwise be stopped—or in case the enemy took the initiative in resorting to tactical nuclear arms.

Compared to some of the more extreme theories, the McNamara doctrine seems moderate and comprehensive. It incorporates the concepts held in common by all the theoreticians, such as non-proliferation, communication between enemies, graduated response, and precautions against escalation, but it neither limits itself to minimum deterrence nor, on the other hand, promotes commitment to counterforce capability at any price or to an extensive civil defense program. Minimum deterrence as defined by the specialists is the capability in any circumstances of inflicting upon an enemy engaged in open aggression such retaliation as he would consider unacceptable. A few hundred invulnerable missiles would suffice for this purpose. But while a minimum capability of this sort may be perfectly adequate for a country without foreign commitments and anxious only to deter attacks against its own territory, it would not meet the needs of a world power such as the United States, forced or determined to conduct global diplomacy.

Thus the Kennedy Administration at the beginning made extensive efforts, not to bridge the (non-existent) missile gap, but rather to insure the sort of indisputable superiority required by the McNamara doctrine. It was aiming at a reserve force capable of countercity strikes following a phase of nuclear exchanges aimed at the retaliatory forces, even if the Soviets took the initiative. But gradually the Administration seemed to accept a progressive decline in strategic counterforce capability without making any attempt to compensate for the loss, either by massive increases in conventional armaments or by a vast civil defense program.

The McNamara doctrine left Europeans more troubled than convinced. It would have made for a measure of uneasiness even if American spokesmen had been clearer in their explanations and Europeans had been able fully to understand it. Moreover, the feeling was partly justified in that the doctrine did, in fact, constitute a response—whether appropriate or not is open to debate—to the novel situation that had been ten years in the making: what one might call the psychologically equal vulnerability of Russia and the United States. Europeans discovered that their security was no longer based on automatic American nuclear response to any Soviet violation of the military line of demarcation but rather on the Russians' uncertainty about United States reaction to an aggressive move on their part.

Nor was this all: the disparity between European and American risks stood out with new clarity. This inequality had been most sharply felt in 1950, when a defenseless Europe served as hostage to the Soviet Union—then itself lacking nuclear retaliatory capability—but gradually it had tended to recede, as an all-out nuclear war unleashed by the Soviet Union, which would have made the United States mainland a prime target, became the sole hypothesis conceivable. In 1958–59, the years when much probably mistaken anxiety centered on the missile gap, and when Wohlstetter raised the specter of a thermonuclear Pearl Harbor, one might have been tempted to agree with the United States senator who said that on the first day, or rather the first minute, of the explosion he would rather be in Europe than in the United States. But it took the McNamara doctrine to force Europeans into realizing that their situation was ultimately not identical with that of the United States and that there was less truth than wishful thinking in the old bromide about all of us being in the same boat.

To begin with, European cities are open to strikes by medium-range missiles, of which the Russians have a large number, while cities in the United States can be hit only by ICBMs, still relatively rare according to United States experts.[4] Furthermore, raising the atomic threshold might, in layman's language, mean that war could be fought on European soil and devastate that continent while the territories of both the

---

[4] If bombers are included in this comparison, European vulnerability is even greater. Only long-range bombers can reach targets on the United States mainland, and this at considerable risk, while fighters and medium-range bombers can easily strike at any target in Europe.

United States and the Soviet Union were spared out of a desire, strategic or moral, to prevent extreme escalation. It has by no means been proved, as we shall see, that the advance consideration of *options* and of a *pause* would in fact increase the probability of operations in which Europeans alone would be the victims, but the mere mention of them tends to make such a situation seem less improbable. In any event, the fact remains that in a crisis all decisions determining the course of hostilities will be made by the President of the United States and his advisers.

Actually this state of affairs should be blamed on geography rather than on the President of the United States; for even in the thermonuclear age distance has not been entirely eliminated as a factor, except in the imagination of so-called experts inclined to confuse strategy with science fiction. Europe's proximity to the presumptive enemy entails increased vulnerability to bombers and missiles. Continental Europe and the Soviet empire share the same land mass, and the common frontier implies at least a theoretical possibility of local aggression with conventional weapons below the atomic threshold. The difference between Continental Europe and Great Britain, which can be attacked only by planes or missiles, is due not to the doctrine of graduated retaliation but to the hard facts of geography, and the same holds true for Western Europe as against the United States, accessible only to long-range bombers or intercontinental missiles. The new doctrine acknowledges this difference, and as long as the United States has on its borders no enemy capable of local aggression, any theories concerning such local operations will apply only to the European segment of the Atlantic Alliance. In the abstract, as presented in the preceding chapter, the doctrine of graduated response may seem eminently reasonable, but considered in its proper historic and geographic context it appears to be a sort of insurance policy. As such, it may be understandable and legitimate from the American point of view but it does not necessarily coincide with the national interest of Frenchmen and Germans because the primary purpose of the policy is to minimize the risk of a big war that might involve the continental United States at the price of putting up with little wars (little, that is, when viewed from across the ocean) in which only Europeans would be killed.

Proponents of this doctrine aggravated the tension it engendered by some of their own statements and decisions. The graduated response has a twofold function, one an aspect of deterrence and the other an aspect of actual use. Now let us imagine a crisis over Berlin, some encroachment by Soviet or East German troops upon Western rights. It would be futile to deal with it by threatening all-out war, but the threat of graduated response is more viable. If a clear distinction had been made between the two types of strategy or the two phases of a crisis, the graduated response might have been defended as a far more effective deterrent in many situations than a total response. But stress on the strategy of use and the incontestable need, once operations had begun, to avoid immediate escalation to extremes led people to believe that deterrence would already have failed. As a result the proponents of the new doctrine indirectly as well as inaccurately implied that the graduated response was less effective, at least at the level of deterrence. Graduated response thus came to be regarded exclusively as a defense against escalation, against the spread of hostilities to Soviet and American territories, rather than being regarded *at the same time* as a means designed to restore psychological *plausibility* to the American deterrent.

Furthermore, the very arguments advanced by proponents of the new doctrine proved, so to speak, more convincing than they were meant to be. The missile gap had been an issue in the 1960 elections, and an important faction in Congress demanded a crash program to increase the number of American ICBMs in operational readiness. But by the end of the first six months of the new administration, the relative strength of Russia and the United States had undergone a miraculous transformation. No longer was there any question of American weakness; on the contrary, United States superiority had grown to the point where counterforce strategy was once again deemed feasible. Soviet superiority in conventional arms had been taken almost as an article of faith ever since 1950; in 1954 NATO commanders were given authority to use tactical nuclear weapons in case of need to stop the "Soviet hordes." But now, in order to justify the new doctrine as well as increased expenditures for conventional arms, American specialists suddenly called the estimate of 175 Soviet divisions a pure fantasy[5] and claimed that the West could re-establish parity at the conventional level without excessive effort. They said that thirty divisions actually on war

[5] Which, incidentally, it does seem to have been.

footing could counter even large-scale Soviet aggression without having to resort to tactical nuclear weapons. The facts and figures here are far too easily adapted to the strategists' pet notions not to arouse suspicion. If American experts are right this time, it means that they were wrong before; and who is to say that tomorrow's crop of experts will not refute those now holding sway?

The Germans, skeptical or obtuse, were moved to insinuate that the number of Soviet divisions had shrunk simply because if it had not, a few Western divisions more or less could not have made any significant difference in the over-all picture. As for the French, they regarded the theory of counterforce strategy and of graduated response primarily as weapons or arguments against independent national deterrents. Since such deterrents cannot, in fact, be used for anything other than attacks on cities, at least for a long time, they would therefore be of value only within the framework of a massive retaliation strategy. Those few Frenchmen who actually understood the American theory of graduated response condemned it out of hand as soon as it proved incompatible with the doctrine of national forces.

The men in charge of American policy have never, to my knowledge, called for massive increases in conventional NATO troops, nor have they ever explicitly urged upon their allies the formation of an Allied army powerful enough to fight a major war without recourse to tactical nuclear weapons. What they did insist upon, especially with the Germans, was that those divisions provided for be actually put in the field and deployed in a manner that made sense from the military point of view—that is, so that no sector was left defenseless, open to invasion and inviting the creation of *faits accomplis*. Although those responsible for United States strategy and diplomacy have never espoused the doctrine in its extreme form—parity at the conventional level and readiness to fight a major war in Europe with only conventional weapons—some theorists did carry the idea that far and urged upon the West a formal commitment never to initiate the use of nuclear arms. Others, while not explicitly voicing withdrawal of nuclear arms, wanted to revise the system of organization and command controlling these weapons so that, instead of being scattered among numerous units, nuclear arms would all be subject to a special command, to avoid any risk of possibly fatal initiatives by officers below the highest rank.

Responsible officials, openly voicing their own ideas, added to these speculations. Nuclear strategy, as we have seen, involves intrinsic antinomies. *It is impossible, by definition, to ward off one danger without thereby automatically increasing another.* If a nation's deterrent forces are invulnerable, it will not fear the enemy's first strike, will not panic in a crisis, and hence will not be tempted to strike the first blow since there is no risk of its being suddenly disarmed. In technical terms, the danger of a pre-emptive strike decreases along with, and in proportion to, the diminishing vulnerability of the retaliatory capability. The pre-emptive strike is a danger to both duelists; hence it is by no means unreasonable for the side that had dispersed and protected its own force to want the enemy to do likewise. This explains Mr. McNamara's publicly voiced hope that the Russians would also bury their

ICBMs in underground sites. On the other hand, if the Russians do follow his advice, the United States will lose its strategic counterforce capability, which is part of its doctrine and possibly essential to the efficacy of whatever deterrence the United States can exert on behalf of its allies. With both deterrents relatively invulnerable, the respective home territories of the duelists are protected as much as possible against a direct attack—as distinct from allied territories shielded only indirectly by the threat of nuclear retaliation. At least in theory a pattern of high-level stability between two invulnerable thermonuclear forces tends to compromise the efficacy of deterrence even in the face of extreme provocation, such as, for instance, an attack against Western Europe. In any event, by intimating in the course of a conversation that invulnerability of the Soviet retaliatory forces was something to be desired rather than feared, Mr. Mc-Namara confirmed the opinion of his European critics that he was far more concerned about American security—bolstered by the elimination of the pre-emptive strike risk—than about Europe, whose safety depends on American strategic counterforce capability. Specialists may realize that McNamara carefully weighed the pros and cons of an invulnerable Soviet thermonuclear system against the advantages of American strategic counterforce capability; hostile critics, however, will harp on the contradictions with either irony or indignation.

Another controversy, apparently technological, evoked acid comment and provided suspicionmongers with fresh material. In 1958–59, following the first sputnik, when Americans were worried about numerical Soviet superiority in intercontinental ballistic missiles, they had installed medium-range Thors and Jupiters in England, Italy, and Turkey. The official decision to retire these missiles[6] was taken, or at least announced, in the spring of 1963, a few months after the Cuban crisis. This immediately led to charges that President Kennedy had promised to withdraw them from Turkey and Italy as part of a bargain involving withdrawal of Soviet missiles from Cuba. United States leaders rightly replied that the move had actually been planned long before and was in line with sound military reasoning: the missiles in question were vulnerable, easily destroyed by the enemy, and hence usable only in a first strike. According to current theory, such weapons *provoke* rather than *deter*. But this sort of argument did not convince all Europeans; for even though the missiles might well be worthless in an all-out war, they still presented a threat to any aggressor contemplating limited operations. They constituted evidence of United States commitment, and no aggressor could destroy them without at the same time killing United States personnel—that is, without incurring a serious risk of reprisals. Therefore these obsolete weapons, useless and perhaps even dangerous within the context of United States global strategy, were nonetheless regarded by the Turks and some Europeans as a contribution to their own security.

In a more general way, the majority of Europeans and General Norstad himself demanded installation on European soil of medium-range missiles to offset

[6] Probably less advanced than Soviet missiles, because they were older models that used liquid fuel, had a long firing delay, and lacked protection.

Soviet ones aimed at Western Europe. Soviet missiles are, after all, stationed in Eastern Europe; why should the defense against them not be launched directly from the lands they menace? General Norstad, NATO Supreme Commander living in Europe among Europeans, was ready to accept this argument, and it seems that his successor, General Lemnitzer, is also inclined to concede its validity.

Here again, within the context of global strategy, Washington's preferences are understandable, although not without some difficulty. United States strategists seem to oppose installation of any missiles on the soil of continental Europe whose range exceeds a few hundred miles, which would establish an additional line of demarcation differentiating between close-range and long-range exchanges. Pointing to United States ground divisions, Air Force squadrons and medium-range missiles as ample proof of inflexible United States commitment, the Americans fail to see why missiles with a range of between 1250 and 1500 miles should be installed on European soil rather than on duly dispersed and detection-proof submarines. But their refusal to do so, as some critics charge, again emphasizes the possibility of limitation, of a differentiation between a war in Europe on the one hand and a war between Russia and the United States on the other. Europeans are not likely to view this implication with anything but apprehension.

These technical discussions were seized upon by the press and blown up into a controversy, in the wake of the Skybolt affair and the subsequent Nassau agreement. Briefly, the British had been counting on the

air-to-ground Skybolt missiles to prolong by another
few years the at least theoretical efficacy of their national deterrent force (subsonic V-bombers). The
Americans had warned them months in advance that
the Skybolt project had run into serious trouble and
would be scrapped because of excessive cost and insufficient yield, but their decision, when finally announced, seemed to come as a stunning surprise both
to the British public and to at least some members of
the government. Actually, in terms of security the consequences were slight; an independent use of the British deterrent is hardly conceivable, and losing the
illusion of an independent force could not have substantially augmented the dangers to which Great Britain is exposed. But psychologically and politically the
British public sustained a hard blow.

The British Government had already given up on
the Bluestreak missile, which had been considered the
key to an independent deterrent, but not before
spending some hundred million pounds in futile attempts to perfect it. If it did not come up with a substitute for the Skybolt, the opposition was bound to
expose and exploit the bankruptcy of Conservative
policies; for the fact was that after ten years and hundreds of millions of pounds Britain still did not have—
or else no longer had—that independent force that
would have assured it a special place of its own on
the international scene.

Constrained to find such a substitute, or at least feel-
ing constrained to do so for reasons of internal politics,
Macmillan vetoed British participation in any United
States efforts to perfect long-range air-to-ground mis-

siles.[7] The two governments finally reached the now famous agreement under which the United States is to turn over Polaris missiles to Great Britain while the latter will produce the submarines and nuclear warheads. The Conservative government, in turn, agreed to take part in a multinational deterrent force, with the British national deterrent to be henceforth integrated in a special NATO command, but without losing its autonomy and subject to withdrawal in the interest of Britain's "supreme national interest." A further point of the agreement concerned a multilateral force consisting of surface vessels carrying Polaris missiles and manned by multinational crews.

Let us take a look at how the three major European powers reacted to the McNamara doctrine and to the problems arising from the Nassau agreement.

British public opinion generally is divided on the issue of nuclear strategy. We may leave aside the *unilateralists,* or advocates of British unilateral disarmament, while bearing in mind that this group continues to exert much influence despite the political defeat it sustained within the Labour party at the hands of Hugh Gaitskell. The pacifism of the British people, evident on numerous occasions between the two World Wars, today manifests itself in opposition to nuclear armament and as such it appeals to millions.

Most of the British analysts—there are not many of them—would subscribe to the American theory, with certain reservations as to details that vary in degree of intensity. The late John Strachey in his last book,

[7] He also turned down shorter-range air-ground missiles.

On the Prevention of War, came out in support of the guiding concepts originated in Cambridge and Santa Monica, which have been adopted by the White House and the Pentagon. He too advocated Western reinforcement in conventional arms, communication between nuclear powers, and maintenance of peace pending the desired but temporarily unrealizable disarmament through concerted action by all members of the nuclear club. (Whatever their differences, these members have a common interest in not using these weapons that does and should prevail.) Alastair Buchan, director of the Institute for Strategic Studies, for his part accepts what is perhaps the most important thesis postulated by American theorists, the need for an Atlantic deterrent subject to unified operational command. Buchan would meet the problem of effective European participation in the conduct of Allied strategy by a reorganization of NATO rather than by a multiplication of national forces or creation of a European force, even though the latter may be technically feasible.

The present positions of the two British parties *appear* to be somewhat as follows, though doubts persist on several points. The Labour party, which rejected unilateral disarmament, remains equally opposed to the formation of the club of non-nuclear powers envisaged by the late Hugh Gaitskell. Harold Wilson, the new party leader, said that for the present he would end all efforts toward an independent deterrent and, in line with American wishes, concentrate instead on conventional forces while at the same time reopening negotiations on the Nassau agreement. But if he actually takes over the government, Mr. Wilson may find that to reverse a policy conducted for the past fifteen years at considerable expense[8] is much more difficult than he now seems to think.

The representatives of the Conservative party speak with two voices. At NATO councils in Paris they perform as the most dedicated proponents of integration and collective action, while back on their own home grounds and in the House of Commons they indulge in some of General de Gaulle's own favorite arguments: that no one can tell what the future will bring, that no great country can afford to be wholly dependent on another for its defense, and that the United States may not always be prepared to protect what Her Majesty's government would regard as vital interests.

It is hard to say which reflects the true ideas of Sir Alec Douglas-Home and Harold Macmillan—the London line with its discreet insistence upon the diminished credibility of United States deterrence due to progressive equalization of thermonuclear strength, or the Paris line with its Atlantic orthodoxy in glaring contrast to the French attitude. I suspect that public abandonment of the independent deterrent is regarded by the Conservative government as practical suicide, even though I doubt that Conservative leaders have any real confidence in the efficacy of such a force vis-à-vis the Soviet Union. What the national deterrent guarantees is not so much British *security* as British *status*. As a result, Macmillan found himself caught in a position where he could neither explicitly justify his military policy because it was based merely on prestige factors, nor yet frankly oppose American ideas be-

[8] If the approximate figure of £200 million annually is correct, this would amount to some £2 billion in ten years.

cause of the "special relationship" he sought to maintain with the United States and, in particular, with the United States Atomic Energy Commission.

This conflict between the desire for a national force on the one hand and the need at least to appear to support the American doctrine on the other became glaringly obvious in connection with the multilateral force. The Conservative government accepted the plan in principle at Nassau, but they have never actually honored this semi-commitment. In October 1963 Britain finally agreed to take part in talks relative to such a force, but without accepting any obligations for the future.

The German Federal Republic was divided on the subject of the McNamara doctrine, in much the same way as was Britain. Official circles generally, and the then Defense Minister Josef Strauss in particular, reacted negatively. On the other hand, the attitude of certain strategic analysts and the official spokesman for the Social Democratic Party was close to that of John Strachey and, consequently, of American theoreticians.

Among the analysts, the best-known defender of the American doctrine is Helmut Schmidt; the title of his book, *Verteidigung oder Vergeltung*, (*Defense or Retaliation*) recalls the title of a book by B. H. Liddell Hart, *Deterrence or Defense*. In common with the opposing school of thought, Schmidt takes as his point of departure the decline of United States deterrent capabilities because of the greater vulnerability of the United States mainland. But he does not believe this decline is exclusively or even chiefly due to the distance between Europe and the United States, to the doctrine of graduated response, or to the inability of one country to protect another simply because no aggressor will ever be convinced that any given country will, when the chips are down, risk incommensurate devastation for the sake of an ally. Instead, Schmidt with uncommon good sense ascribes the decline above all to the ever increasing monstrosity of the nuclear weapons themselves and to the magnitude of destruction henceforth possible. The Americans, so the argument runs, are not going to sacrifice New York and Boston for London and Paris. This may well be true, but will the French sacrifice Paris for Hamburg, or, for that matter, all of France for the sake of one city or one province? In other words, unless the aggressor began with an all-out assault, he would not be likely to provoke an all-out response, even if he were to attack the very country that itself controls the deterrent. Every nuclear power must be capable of raising the atomic threshold—that is, it must acquire a certain defensive capability—because lacking one, it may eventually find itself confronted by a choice between suicide and surrender, a choice that constitutes the inexorable result of blind reliance on a threat whose credibility is constantly declining.

The United States was forced to give up the doctrine of massive retaliation; European nations acquiring national deterrents—i.e., limited and vulnerable forces—will have to follow suit for identical and even more compelling reasons. Mr. Ehrler and the Social Democrats seem inclined toward this view, the practical implementation of which would point toward Western reinforcement in conventional arms—that is, parity at all levels.

The opposite point of view was presented in equally radical terms by Albert Weinstein, military columnist of the *Frankfurter Allgemeine Zeitung,* a journalist generally assumed to reflect the opinions of Josef Strauss. His fundamental point is not the decline of American deterrence, but Western inability to offset the conventional forces of the Soviet Union. Highly industrialized nations such as those of Western Europe, with urbanized populations accustomed to relatively high standards of living and comfort, will never be able to hold their own in ground warfare against armies recruited from among people still half primitive. Furthermore, after the shock of the last war, the Germans are now anxious not to limit but rather to prevent hostilities altogether. Any military operations conducted on German soil, even if concluded swiftly and without territorial losses, pose a mortal threat to the morale of the nation and to the very existence of the Federal Republic.

It would indeed be difficult to conceive of any war less than total, where the German Federal Republic is concerned. The entire country is about half the size of France, and what from the perspective of Washington, D.C., might look like limited operations would be an all-out war as far as Bonn is concerned. Most analysts therefore agree that the real conflict of national interest built into the Atlantic Alliance pits the German Federal Republic against the United States. Both want to prevent any war, big or little; but Germany, on the front line, is reluctant to accept a strategy which, by reducing the chances of escalation, increases those of minor aggression, while the United States, removed by several thousand miles from the potential theater of ground operations, is determined to prevent escalation even at the cost of what, from that distance, appear to be mere minor skirmishes.

We may concede this theoretical conflict of interest; it still leaves open the question of which strategy would most effectively meet the danger of "minor aggression," for the arguments proffered by Albert Weinstein could serve with equal logic to justify either graduated response or massive retaliation. It would surely be the height of paradox to assert that the West *would weaken its deterrent capability in relation to local aggression by acquiring the means to repel such aggression without recourse to nuclear weapons.*

Mr. Weinstein's argument, if I understand it correctly, rejects all such distinctions as futile sophistry. According to him, the day the shooting starts, each nation will commit all its resources to battle as states have always done throughout history whenever their national interest was at stake, without paying the slightest attention to subtle gradations of strategy worked out in the ivory towers of institutes or universities. Granted this premise, any effort to stress in advance the wide range of intermediary steps between the first shot fired from a conventional gun and the explosion of the first nuclear device would have no effect other than to make the enemy question Western determination. It would not in any significant way help to reduce the probability of escalation once the threshold of violence had in fact been crossed.

Let us temporarily sum up this controversy—at present altogether theoretical—by concluding that the effects of the doctrine of graduated response upon deterrence depend on the potential aggressor's inter-

pretation of it and on the advance measures taken by
the defenders. The aggressor may, in fact, read it either as an expression of fear and retreat in the face
of impending danger or, on the contrary, as a rational
organization of deterrence on all levels and hence as
proof of strong and intelligent determination. His interpretation may hinge on whether or not application
of the doctrine seems plausible; for instance, whoever
proclaims his resolve initially to use only conventional
arms will court the danger of disastrous misunderstandings unless he first acquires such arms in sufficient
quantities. A promise not to initiate the use of nuclear
arms is credible only if the means to keep it are manifestly available; otherwise the signals will cancel each
other out, words conveying intentions contradicted by
deeds or the absence thereof. What conclusions the
other side would draw from this silent dialogue is anyone's guess.

But if German reaction to the McNamara doctrine
was lukewarm—especially since Chancellor Adenauer
did not seem altogether unaffected by the suspicions
of those who saw it as the first step toward American
disengagement, at least atomic disengagement—the
Bonn government, including the new Defense Minister von Hassel (who in the meantime had succeeded
Josef Strauss) was quick to approve the Nassau accord.

Under the Treaty of Paris, the Bonn Republic had
agreed not to manufacture atomic, bacteriological or
chemical warfare weapons. It has no sites available
for testing atomic or nuclear devices. In direct border-
line contact with the Soviet bloc and dependent for
its security on the vast but distant power of the United

States, it is supposed to supply a substantial number of ground divisions. A nuclear program for military uses would require an enormous increase in the defense budget, inconceivable under present conditions; moreover, such a program would run headlong into the double veto of both Russia and the United States. An independent deterrent, therefore, is out of the question; but the offer of a multilateral force gave Bonn leaders a chance to become more familiar with the rudiments of nuclear strategy. The Federal Republic was given the right to participate in General Staff work and in the planning and elaboration of strategy. The multilateral force officially remains an integral part of the Atlantic force, subject to the operational command of the President of the United States; but this arrangement merely reflects the realities of the current situation. Ten years hence it may well have changed. If Europe achieves an authentic political union, the man in the White House may no longer cling quite so adamantly to the American veto.

None of the reasons that moved the Bonn government to welcome the Nassau agreement and the idea of a multilateral force held any attraction for the French. France had embarked on a military atomic program. She has A-bombs, first-generation delivery vehicles (Mirage IV), and a plant for isotope separation under construction at Pierrelatte. In his press conference of January 14, 1963, General de Gaulle expressed himself on the subject with vigor and clarity: "France has noted the Anglo-American Bahamas agreement. It will unquestionably come as no surprise to anyone that we cannot subscribe to it as conceived. It would indeed be pointless for us to buy Polaris rockets while we lack both the submarines from which to launch them and the thermonuclear warheads with which to arm them. Undoubtedly the day will come when we shall have both submarines and warheads. But it is a long time off. The World War, the invasion and its consequences have held us back considerably in the field of atomic development. But once we do have these submarines and warheads, of what use will the Polaris be to us? By that time we shall probably have rockets of our own design. In other words, technically speaking, for us the matter is not, as one might say, 'of topical relevance.' Furthermore, it does not conform to the principle I just mentioned, of having and controlling our own deterrent. To dissipate our means in a multilateral force under foreign command would be contrary to this principle of our defense and of our policy."

The technical arguments are unquestionably valid. But the Nassau agreement, which implicitly put France on the same footing as Great Britain, was not being presented as final and forever immutable; it could have served as an opening for further negotiations. But General de Gaulle decided otherwise, as could have been predicted. He probably did not feel that the time was right for French-American negotiations, and his aim—total independence of the French deterrent—is incompatible with the American objective of preserving the unity of the Atlantic command over atomic or thermonuclear arms.

The arguments cited by General de Gaulle in favor of the independent deterrent are familiar for the most part and have been used by many a commentator. "Deterrence is now a Russian as well as an American fact, which means that in the event of an all-out atomic war horrible destruction will inevitably ensue for both countries. In these circumstances no one alive can say whether, where, how and to what extent American nuclear arms would be used in the defense of Europe."

The formulation itself is not a felicitous one, for the purpose of atomic weapons is not to "defend" a country but rather to deter the aggressor from attacking. Once it came to using them, the "defense" of Europe by atomic weapons would be tantamount to total destruction. But the French chief of state alludes to the decline of the American deterrent due to the vulnerability of continental United States (always the ultimate point in arguments of this sort) without asking himself whether the French force would be able to compensate for this decline; in other words, whether it could succeed in deterring the enemy where American power had failed to do so.

The manifest confusion between deterrence and defense also makes the entire section of de Gaulle's speech devoted to the Cuban affair rather difficult to understand. "The Americans, finding themselves exposed to direct atomic attack from the Caribbean, took measures designed to meet this threat and, if necessary, to crush it; neither they nor, for that matter, anyone else believed that the showdown would necessarily involve Europe, and they did not resort to direct European help. On the other hand, the forces that they immediately decided to use in order to meet a direct attack, whether launched only from Cuba or combined with another attack originating elsewhere, were automatically assigned to functions other than the defense of Europe, even if Europe itself had been attacked in turn." The idea that weapons assigned to a Caribbean conflict would have had to be withdrawn from Europe makes no sense whatsoever in the context of atomic strategy either in the phase of deterrence or in that of actual use. The determination displayed in the Caribbean served to reinforce the deterrent covering Europe, the more so since the entire military apparatus of the United States throughout the world was in a state of alert. If it had come to their actual use, the stock of tactical nuclear weapons which the United States maintained in Europe would have proved ample, so that any possible commitment of nuclear devices in a Caribbean war from stockpiles within the United States proper would in no way have denuded the defenses of Europe. The real danger pointed up by the Cuban crisis was an altogether different one: that Europe may become embroiled in a conflict sparked in some distant corner of the globe. But how can one benefit from an alliance without paying the price? The benefit gained is protection by a strong ally. The price is running the risks involved in the protection of that ally's interests.

As to the circumstances in which the French deterrent would have its own efficacy as distinct from the American force, General de Gaulle hardly hinted at them in the course of that same press conference. "In 1945," he said, "two then rudimentary bombs persuaded Japan to surrender because it was unable to reply in kind. I do not here wish to evoke the hypothetical circumstances in which Europe may be subject to nuclear actions which, though localized, would have enormous political and psychological consequences unless there existed the certainty that retaliation on the same scale would immediately be unleashed." Here again the example is poorly chosen, indicating no very profound thought about contemporary problems. At the time the two bombs were dropped on Hiroshima and Nagasaki, Japan had already lost the war, and a peace party had for months been trying to make contact with Washington. Among all the hypothetical circumstances imaginable, that of "localized nuclear actions" (a bomb on Hamburg or on Dusseldorf) happens to be the most unlikely, because it would compel the United States to respond by at least equivalent action. And furthermore, if in the present context the Soviet leaders are not deterred from "localized nuclear actions" by the American deterrent, what reason do they have to fear French retaliation? The argument is therefore doubly defective; it postulates a highly implausible situation in which, moreover, the French deterrent would be absolutely worthless.

General de Gaulle himself has not explicitly taken part in the controversy over total versus graduated response, at least not in public.[9] But a vulnerable national deterrent, effective only against cities, must logically lead to the advocacy of total response. The French doctrine of deterrence is a fatal rehash of the massive retaliation concept, and it is a miniature version ten years behind the times.

General de Gaulle's decision, while it may be propped up by arguments, is ultimately based on his own philosophy, which equates the state with national defense. "If a country like France has to go to war, it must be *her* war. The effort must be *her* effort. Otherwise, our country would be denying everything

[9] In the military councils of the Alliance, the French representatives are regarded as theoretically favoring all-out response.

it has stood for from its beginnings, its role, its self-esteem, its soul. . . . The system of integration is finished."[10] To what extent this traditional philosophy, evolved during four or five centuries of national absolutism, still applies today when war, unlike the wars of the past, would utterly destroy the essence of the nation, is certainly debatable. The soul of France will survive peace, even a peace safeguarded by an integrated force; it will not survive a war, French though that war may be to the core. In short, in the atomic age everything, including the age-old desire for independence, must be subordinated to the contemporary needs of security.[11]

It is true that "one can potentially destroy France from any point on the globe," and that hence "our force must be so designed as to be able to go into action anywhere on the globe." But this fact, though it may explain the objective, still does not enable us to attain it, at least not within the next fifteen years.

[10] Speech at the Ecole Militaire, November 3, 1959.
[11] Which does not mean that the desire for independence should be completely disregarded.

4

The Independent French Deterrent

Both proponents and opponents of an independent French nuclear deterrent are as a rule passionate and categorical in voicing their views, based in both cases largely on theoretical positions. Thus it is self-evident, for example, that Gaullist rejection of an integrated force logically implies advocacy of the French atomic program, regardless of consequences or results. On the other hand, pacifists, who, pending total disarmament, want at least to eliminate atomic weapons, obviously oppose their proliferation.

As happens all too often, the most reputable experts tend to juggle the most debatable figures. M. Jules Moch, in a press conference held on behalf of the *Ligue Nationale contre la Force de Frappe* (National League against the Striking Force) asserted that a single H-bomb would devastate 7800 squares miles (20,000 km²) and kill an average of 200,000 in the Soviet Union (with a population density of ten) and 1,700,000 in France (with a population density of eighty-five). Now it is simply not true that just any H-bomb would devastate 7800 square miles. In a report published by the United States Atomic Energy Commission on October 1, 1961, calculations were based on

a 100-megaton bomb; the range of major blast destruction was estimated at up to 18.125 miles, with incendiary effects covering 1000 square miles. Fire may
possibly extend the range of destruction up to sixty
miles and cover 11,300 square miles. But at present
neither of the Big Two possesses 100-megaton bombs,
and the estimates of incendiary effects are still controversial. The range of severe blast damage for a 20-
megaton bomb would be eight or ten miles, according
to official estimates, or ten times greater than that of a
20-kiloton bomb in return for a thousand times more
power. According to these figures, the range of surface destruction due to blast should be in the hundreds rather than thousands of square miles. It is true,
of course, that damage will extend beyond the "range
of severe destruction," but, even so, the equation of
"one H-bomb = 7800 square miles destroyed" is in no
way valid, given presently available official data.[1]

Moreover, the estimate of casualties in terms of population density is also fallacious. It would be valid
only on the assumption that bombs are dropped at
random on enemy territory; if they are aimed at cities,
the relevant factor will be density of urban rather than
general population.

Such inflated estimates, far from serving the cause
to which Jules Moch and the *Ligue Nationale contre
la Force de Frappe* are devoting their efforts, offer
their foes a chance to strike a blow on behalf of their
own diametrically opposite thesis. If "thirty thermonuclear projectiles are enough to destroy France," it
follows that any country in possession of thirty ther-

[1] M. Moch may have been thinking of radiation rather than
thermal or blast effects, but even then his figures are debatable.

monuclear devices could inflict upon any other country, regardless of size and—given the existence of intercontinental rockets—regardless of location, damage at least equal in scope to that to which it is itself exposed."[2] Taking one further step and confusing the present with a hypothetical future, General P.-M. Gallois decrees that "thermonuclear weapons neutralize the armed masses, equalize the factors of demography, contract distance, level the heights, limit the advantages which until yesterday the Big Powers derived from the sheer dimensions of their territory (space to retreat into) . . ." And finally: "It is easy to prove that countries as different as Switzerland and Communist China are in the same boat when it comes to the nuclear threat." According to Jules Moch, a great power needs its territory more than ever in the thermonuclear age, while for General Gallois the very opposite holds true—territorial dimensions are no longer of any importance. The two theses refute each other by their very exaggerations; size of territory still counts, whether the problem is to test bombs, to assure survival of part of the population, or to disperse reprisal weapons.[3] It is considerably more difficult to

[2] "Le Monde Diplomatique" by P.-M. Gallois, April 1963, reprinted in *Pour ou Contre la Force de Frappe*, Les Editions John Didier, 6, rue Garancière, Paris VI.

[3] In his article of April 1963 in the *Revue de Défense Nationale* as well as in the *Tribune Libre du Monde* (July 28–29, 1963), P.-M. Gallois attributed to R. E. Lapp the opinion that it would take forty Soviet missiles to destroy one hard U. S. missile. "On the basis of Dr. Lapp's calculations, if the U. S. had 1000 missiles installed in silos, the Soviets would have to launch against them a salvo of 40,000 nuclear missiles. They probably have no more than 200 at present." ("La Nouvelle politique extérieure des Etats-Unis et la Sécurité de l'Europe," *Revue de Défense Nationale*, April 1963, p. 573, Note 1.) R. E. Lapp in his book *Kill and Overkill* (1963) said nothing of the sort.

hit industrial centers scattered over thousands of miles than those bunched together in clusters. And how many years will it take until a country like France is able to launch thirty thermonuclear projectiles in a second-strike blow against a Big Power? Even assuming it can be done, what is the ratio of cost to yield?

To conclude these quotations, here is a sample from the oratory of Michel Debré, who ended a fairly rational but superficial discussion with the following categorical statement: "The conclusion is clear, and there is no point playing games with it. We might even say that we simply have no other choice unless we are prepared to surrender all political autonomy, all influence in international life, all scientific ambition in the world of tomorrow, and all military defense in general."[4] This might lead his readers to believe that Great Britain had derived enormous benefits from her national deterrent over the last ten years, when in actual fact the course of her diplomatic efforts during that period was a series of unmitigated failures. Is it true that continental Europe or France would have no autonomy, no influence on international relations, if they were to become part of an integrated Atlantic system of deterrence? The vigor of M. Debré's asser-

---

"Given a circular error probability of one mile and a ten mega-ton warhead, the enemy could destroy our hard Atlas and Titan sites with a few hundred missiles." P. 73. In the May issue of *Bulletin of the Atomic Scientists*, Dr. Lapp wrote that estimates have varied from "several" (November 1962) to eight (McNamara, January 1963). "I myself," he continued, "have publicly stated during the past four years that we must expect even the hard sites to become soft in proportion to the increase in enemy ICBM's. For this very reason I personally believe that our hard Minutemen are not a good national investment."

4 *Au Service de la Nation,* Paris, 1963, p. 158.

tions is surpassed only by the insubstantiality of his proofs. Or is it, rather, that this impassioned Jacobin must always find an outlet for his zeal, and that French deterrence will have to serve the purpose now that he no longer has Algeria?

To take a definite and immutable stand for or against a national deterrent in the abstract makes very little sense. The national deterrent represents one of several possible ways of allocating scarce resources; hence the most satisfactory method of arriving at a thoughtful and, if not rational, at least reasoned decision is the economist's approach, in terms of the criterion of marginal utility.

What are the various types of return—advantages and disadvantages, or positive and negative returns— to be expected from armaments to which a given amount has been allocated? (For the sake of simplifying matters, let us assume the 1963 figure for France to be 20 billion francs.) The most obvious return, sometimes the only one referred to by both defense and prosecution, is *security,* or rather the contribution that a given type of weapon makes to security. An analysis exclusively in terms of security, however, is bound to give a false slant to the data under consideration; at least three other dimensions must be added: *the influence on the ally* or *autonomy within the alliance,*[5] *prestige on the international scene,* and, finally, the consequences that a particular program will

---

[5] Influence and autonomy do not necessarily go together. France might conceivably have more influence on U. S. strategy if she were to abandon her Lone Ranger role.

have for *economic development* and especially for *scientific progress.*[6]

The controversy has focused on the contribution to security. But here again it has been largely distorted by terms of reference confined almost exclusively to the first-generation deterrent. Proponents of the French force stubbornly insist on trying to prove the deterrent value of fifty Mirage IV bombers, a preposterous stunt that leaves them wide open in any discussion. General Gallois, somewhat less naïve, demonstrates in numerous articles that a small retaliatory capability would be sufficient to deter one of the Big Powers, but for purposes of this demonstration he always somehow conjures up a small and *relatively invulnerable* force, one whose destruction would present serious problems. He ends up proving that in the *world of tomorrow* there will no longer be any difference between Switzerland and China, thanks to the equalizing power of the atom, but he does not go so far as to claim that in the *world of today* Soviet bombers or medium-range missiles could not wipe out most of the Mirage IV bombers or that the few that might conceivably survive could go on to penetrate fully alerted Soviet defenses.

Let us examine a force consisting of fifty Mirage IV bombers in terms of strategy of deterrence as well as strategy of use. Obviously this force is not intended to deter some African or Asian country, both because the planes lack the requisite range and because in the

[6] This list is not necessarily complete. The atomic weapon may have been conceived as a means to reconcile the army to the loss of the empire, or to restore France's confidence in her destiny.

present context of international relations the atomic weapon cannot be used in Africa, not even as an instrument of diplomacy. In Europe, the French force is of necessity complementary to the American deterrent, and the scope of its contribution to security must therefore be measured by the extent to which it would be capable of deterring the Soviet Union from acts of aggression that the combined (Anglo-American) force had failed to inhibit. I must confess that I find such a situation between now and 1970 hard to imagine.

Whether it is a matter of massive conventional attacks or limited atomic actions, the Soviet Union (assuming that it would contemplate either, which under present world conditions is highly improbable) would be deterred far more effectively by the combined Atlantic organization than by the French force alone. This, therefore, leaves local aggression, conducted with conventional arms, which the Americans would be unable to deter but which the existence of a small French force would stop the Kremlin from committing. The argument may not be entirely devoid of merit— who can ever be absolutely sure of anything, in speculations of this sort? But once again, it rather strains the imagination.

By taking the initiative and sending all available Mirage IV bombers—about thirty at the most, since some will always be out of commission at any given time—against Soviet cities, the French Government would deliberately accept in advance the doom of the entire French nation, the inevitable response to whatever damage may have been inflicted by the A-bombs dropped from these planes. And how many planes would actually be able to penetrate Soviet defenses?

That question may be left for the experts to argue about, while we confine ourselves to the fact that the principal Soviet cities are ringed by numerous ground-to-air missiles installations, that the Sam III has a good chance of detecting and downing even low-flying bombers, that furthermore the Mirage IV with a ceiling of about 50,000 feet is not made for hedgehopping and that few, if any, would be likely to return from their mission. Given these facts, Soviet leaders would find it very hard to believe that the government of a country so transparently vulnerable, and without even a trace of civil defense, would deliberately choose to unleash the holocaust in full awareness of the vast discrepancy between what it could inflict and what in turn would be inflicted upon it. A French government trying with this sort of force to deter Soviet leaders from actions from which American power would not deter them would be able to convey to them nothing but a convincing impression of its own insanity. In other words, the deterrence would be effective only within the framework of the so-called "rationality of the irrational." A chief of state with a small nuclear force at his disposal could manifest such blind intransigence, such manifest indifference to danger and to the voice of reason alike, such obstinate determination, that in the end both enemies and friends might uneasily come to believe him capable of bringing down the ultimate catastrophe on all of them. Is General de Gaulle the man able to play this particular role? In any case no successor now in sight could hope to fill his shoes and aspire to the same sort of rather equivocal glory.

We have started with the assumption most favorable to the partisans of a French deterrent—i.e., not the abstract model of a small against a big power but rather a clash within the context of a confrontation between the two blocs. If France with her Mirage IV bombers were to face the Soviet Union all alone, the latter could clearly wipe out all or most of the French delivery vehicles even if they were to be duly dispersed; and if for argument's sake we assume that a few Mirage IV were actually able to penetrate Soviet defenses, how many of them could take off from a country devastated by one or two dozen thermonuclear explosions? What would be left of the communications network? Of the chain of command? And if some planes did manage to get off the ground, what would be their chances of reaching the target? In other words, unless the French force were protected by the threat of American retaliation, it would not hold any deterrent value whatsoever vis-à-vis the Soviet Union.

General Gallois, while conceding that the Soviets could, in fact, destroy the French force, objects that they would not do so without at the same time destroying a good part of France. I agree; and indeed I cannot imagine that the Soviet Union would do this. But if the purpose of the deterrent is merely to "challenge" a big power, then a conventional force that could be overcome only by massive assault would do almost as well. The function of thermonuclear arms is destruction rather than conquest, and there are two ways of parrying their threat. One is to acquire the means of retaliation; the other is to answer intimidation by a refusal to surrender, thus challenging the big power to carry out its insane threat and destroy what it wants

to conquer. Retaliation is beyond the capability of
the French first-generation so-called deterrent; the
alternative, however, depends more on the government, the nation, and the diplomatic context than on
possession of a few bombs.

With its wholly insignificant, not to say non-existent,
contribution to deterrence, the French force worries
our partners,[7] at least the American theorists, precisely because it can be used for nothing but a first
strike; its extreme vulnerability will make it that much
more difficult for a French government to keep cool
in a crisis. But there is more to it. If countercity strategy is to be regarded only as a last resort, it will be
applied solely and exclusively in the final phase; and
when it comes to destroying cities, American power is
such as to make any French assistance wholly irrelevant. In a strategy of rational use, as conceived by the
American analysts, there is not and cannot be room for
a vulnerable French force effective only in attacks
against cities. Such feeble deterrence as it may exert
is based on the assumption of a massive retaliation
strategy—that is, an immediate all-out blow against
the entire vital complex of the enemy. The Russians
would certainly have a hard time believing that a
French government could in cold blood choose to commit national suicide; if, however, this suspicion did
cross their minds, they would be even less inclined to
exercise the sort of restraint that is absolutely essential
if ultimate escalation is to be averted. This is why the
American theorists regard the French force as more

[7] A worry quite as misplaced as the self-confidence of French
dogmatists. If U. S. strategists fear a French pre-emptive strike,
the Russians may also.

of a danger than an asset to France, to the Atlantic Alliance, and to mankind as a whole.

If one's attitude toward the French deterrent depended exclusively on evaluation of the security yield afforded by fifty Mirage IV bombers, the decision could hardly be in doubt; the first-generation French deterrent is unable to retaliate, and its contribution to the American deterrent is insignificant, based as it is on nothing more substantial than a sinister comedy of irrationality. But this does not finish the argument, because the security yield is not the sole criterion; furthermore, the alternative choices extend by implication well beyond 1970.

Within the Alliance itself the effort to acquire a national deterrent has not been altogether futile. Not that France can now, by threatening to trigger a nuclear catastrophe, force the United States to accept her choice of demarcation lines or positions to be defended; but the French ambition to have a national deterrent has nonetheless succeeded in modifying to some extent the attitude of our American ally. Since most of the arms available were theirs, they considered it perfectly normal—as nations always have through the ages—to decide the strategy of the Alliance all on their own, or very nearly so. It was French readiness to assume the enormous burden of an atomic program that helped to make the Kennedy Administration realize the need to strengthen co-operation and to share information within the Alliance if it is to be kept from disintegrating.

One thing should be made clear: the degree of influence exerted within the Alliance is not proportional to the number of bombs and delivery vehicles in the possession of a given country. Great Britain[8] does not seem to have exerted any special influence on the United States except in the matter of atomic negotiations with the Soviet Union. When it came to issues such as the Middle East, the Common Market, or the free trade zone, Britain derived no visible benefits from her thermonuclear bombs and V-bombers. General de Gaulle did not wait for his own deterrent to become operational before proceeding to veto Britain's admission to the Common Market. At the very most it might be said that an independent French deterrent will strengthen the hand of those Americans eager to cut foreign entanglements and fall back on the "Fortress America." French nuclear weapons can have two possible effects on French-American relations within the broader international context: they can either modify American doctrines in a sense deemed more in line with Europe's best interests or else motivate U. S. leaders to keep more aloof from Europe so as not to commit their country unconditionally to the support of an ally who refuses to submit to a common discipline. For those who believe that at the present time America's solemn commitment remains the best guarantee of any real security, this second possibility—an argument in favor of the national deterrent in the eyes of those clamoring for partial or complete U. S. withdrawal—in fact constitutes the strongest argument against it. The security yield of the French deterrent will be negative rather than

[8] At the time of the Korean War, British influence, such as it was, owed nothing to atomic weapons, which Britain had not yet acquired. At the time of Dienbienphu the British may have exerted pressure against U. S. intervention, but I rather doubt that their H-bomb played any role in this one way or the other.

positive if it tends to weaken or sever the links between Europe and America.

The effects of France's nuclear weapons on her international prestige are equally difficult to assess. If France goes ahead with atmospheric tests in defiance of a nuclear test ban signed by the Big Three, she will find herself formally condemned by the vast majority of United Nations members. Even the former French colonies would find it difficult to support the country to which they are still linked by ties of language, culture and friendship. But such vociferous moral indignation would not necessarily imply that the return in terms of prestige is all negative; indignation by no means excludes admiration. A country that acquires those weapons, however belatedly, despite or perhaps because of the invectives hurled at it will be regarded as one of the big powers of this world.

A final consideration involves the scientific progress spurred by construction of the Pierrelatte reactor plant, or by the production of thermonuclear bombs. It is perfectly obvious that when it comes to French industry and economy, the returns on investments in the atomic program are of quite a different order from those on investment in mere military manpower. But the balance of accounts, so unequivocally on the credit side of the ledger as long as we confine our bookkeeping to a comparison between Pierrelatte on the one hand and army barracks on the other, becomes considerably more complex the moment we begin to wonder about alternative employment for those scientists and technicians now drained off by the nuclear program. According to M. Pompidou, "to abandon the atomic effort is to condemn France to becoming an underdeveloped country within the next ten or fifteen years."[9] The statement happens to be a foolish piece of inanity in any event, for even if atomic energy were to replace other sources of power within the next twenty years, the necessary installations could probably be acquired at a cost much below that involved in our own autonomous efforts at discovery and production. But there is also nothing to prevent us from channeling substantial amounts into atomic research for civilian use; are we to assume that the National Assembly would vote down appropriations for peaceful uses of atomic energy and that therefore it takes the H-bomb to make them approve these funds, so that all research becomes an integral part of the French deterrent? In the reign of Charles de Gaulle the mere possibility of such parliamentary intractibility could not be seriously entertained for even one moment.

There are other factors. The atomic program devours a great deal more money (about ten times more) than the entire budget of the National Science Research Committee.[10] An honest balance sheet would require weighing the indisputable assets represented by Pierrelatte, by the nuclear submarine and by the H-bomb against the debits—i.e., the impediments and delays suffered by other areas of scientific research and development as a result of concentrating personnel and funds on the deterrent. Personally I do not feel qualified to make such an audit.

The proponents keep insisting that a program of conventional arms would prove even more costly. This

[9] National Assembly, May 14, 1963.
[10] About 350 million.

is true if the destructive power of nuclear arms is simply measured against that of conventional ones. No
weapon can possibly compete with the H-bomb when
it comes to killing millions of people at the lowest
cost per person. To say that the conventional arms
program advocated by our allies would be even more
expensive is meaningless, because we would ourselves
determine the size of allocations even if we agreed
not to manufacture the atom bombs that no one asked
us to acquire, since no one considers our deterrent a
substantial contribution to common security. One may
readily accept the fact, pointed out by M. Alain Peyrefitte, that an armored division costs three hundred billion old francs, or twice the cost of fifty Mirage IV
bombers. But all this proves is that a modern army
requires vast resources, which happens to be a truism.
And since France cannot do without a minimum of
conventional armed forces, the question arises whether
a second-generation deterrent, given the finite limits
of the national defense budget, is at all compatible
with this indispensable minimum of army divisions,
warships, and airplanes of all types.

The first problem, in fact, raised by the second-
generation deterrent is one of cost and of the extent
to which this cost is compatible with even the most
minimal modernization of the armed forces. Plans call
for the completion by 1972–73 of three nuclear submarines, each equipped with a battery of missiles comparable to the Polaris (of which there are sixteen in
every American nuclear submarine). But some five
years before we ever finish our three submarines, the
Americans will have forty-one. One would really have

to have an exceedingly low estimate of American determination and at the same time be unduly impressed by French willingness to commit suicide in order to believe that her own three submarines will offer France a greater security than that provided by forty-one American vessels. No one can predict exactly how much these submarines and missiles are going to cost. According to Peyrefitte, each Polaris-equipped submarine comes to 800 million new francs, or $160,000,-000. But even if we accept this as the figure given in the budget or as the price at which these ships would be sold to the allies, it still remains difficult accurately to estimate the past, present, and future cost of research, development, and maintenance. It is equally rash to quote a 12-million-dollar figure[11] or Polaris missiles, because the proportion of design and development cost included in the price is not known. Even according to present estimates the second-generation French deterrent will absorb about 25 per cent of the French budget from 1964 to 1969, and there is nothing to indicate that this fraction will actually prove sufficient to permit construction of three nuclear submarines as well as of Polaris-type missiles and the miniaturized nuclear warheads adaptable to them. In fact, a comparison between French estimates and U. S. figures makes this seem rather doubtful; and yet even these low estimates jeopardize programs *regarded as minimal* in the area of conventional arms.

Let us now suppose that the technical and financial obstacles have been overcome and that between now and 1972–73 France succeeds on her own in producing

[11] C. Rougeron, op. cit., p. 72.

these submarines, missiles, and warheads by spending an annual average of between 4.5 and 5 billion francs.[12] A further problem to be solved would be the perfection, between now and 1972, of an anti-missile missile, especially one effective against missiles armed with medium-power warheads such as the present Polaris.[13] Let us suppose that this, too, has been overcome; what, in terms of security, would be the return on the second-generation French deterrent?

In one respect it is likely to be much greater than that of the first-generation force in that the deterrent will be less vulnerable and its delivery vehicles far more difficult to intercept. But vulnerable it will still be, just the same; a force consisting of three submarines can hardly ever keep more than one vessel out at sea at a time; the others, back at their bases for repair or maintenance, will be as vulnerable there as the Mirage IV bombers are on the ground. Furthermore, if it were not for the few dozen U. S. submarines, the lone French one would be wholly without protection. What retaliation could France threaten in the event of its sudden and mysterious disappearance? In fact, the relative invulnerability of our three submarines would essentially be a function of the American force. Left to themselves, these vessels would still constitute only a very weak deterrent.

Moreover, what tends to be overlooked is that even

[12] The figure is based on the assumption that the deterrent will absorb *on the average* 20 per cent of a 20-billion-franc budget, which means 40 per cent of the arms procurement part of the total budget. This percentage, in 1964, already appears too low an estimate.

[13] The warheads of the first Polaris were 500 kilotons. The latest models have a greater range (1600 to 2000 miles) and a more powerful warhead.

if the submarines successfully escape detection, the deterrent as such remains vulnerable to the extent to which the systems of early warning, command, and communications on shore are liable to destruction by the enemy's first strike. If the submarine at sea is to launch the retaliatory strike, orders to this effect must first be issued, communicated, and received.

The construction of underground command posts, the maintenance of radio communications in the event of nuclear exchanges, and the technological requirements incidental to operating the French second-generation deterrent present problems incomparably more hazardous and complex than is suggested by that comic-strip notion of three submarines lurking in the ocean depths, ready at a moment's notice to hurl death at the cities of any enemy encroaching upon the security of France.

But this is not yet all. Even if we were to assume the most favorable circumstances, with all obstacles duly disposed of and all technological problems solved, it still would seem doubtful, to put it mildly, that a force consisting of three submarines could reach the point beyond which the so-called theory of proportional deterrence would apply with even a shred of probability. I try never to oversimplify the argument. It is a fact that the United States spent 15 billion dollars for its deterrent in a single year (1962–63); it would manifestly take some sort of miracle if France, fifteen years late in getting started and spending only one fifteenth that amount, were to put together a deterrent worthy of the name. And yet this objection, taken by itself, is not wholly convincing because in this area the rule of proportionality may lead to the wrong conclusions. The American force vastly exceeds the minimum required for deterrence; its purpose is to permit a wide range of strategic uses, while a small independent force would be tailored strictly to the demands of so-called minimum deterrence.

Even so, the three submarines, though less vulnerable than the Mirage IV bombers, and with improved reprisal capability, would probably still remain below what René Schmitt, with good sense, refers to as "the critical power."[14] I shall refrain from assigning any precise figure to this "threshold of efficacy" of a deterrent force; it has by no means been proved that a small country, in order to deter a big one, must have a capability equal to 20 per cent of the latter's deterrent. But the three French submarines of 1972 will represent neither 20 per cent of the Soviet force, as stipulated by René Schmitt, nor yet 10 per cent of the American force as foolishly decreed by Alain Peyrefitte, who estimates that by 1970 France will have 200 thermonuclear devices as against America's 2000. (Adding a zero to the latter figure would probably bring him closer to the factual state of affairs.[15]) What matters is not so much the ratio of the French to either the Soviet or the American force as the absolute destructive capability that may rightfully and legitimately be attributed to the French deterrent. This capability will be so limited, and the fate of France in the event

[14] *Pour ou Contre la Force de Frappe*, p. 231.
[15] Comparing the numbers of "devices" is ambiguous in any event; if the term refers to bombs, shells, and warheads, the United States has tens of thousands. If the numbers of delivery vehicles are to be compared, the 1 to 10 ratio is again ludicrous, since the 41 U. S. submarines alone contain more than ten times the number of "devices" carried by the three French submarines.

of a thermonuclear war so inconceivably frightful, that it would again be very hard to imagine any Soviet moves that a French force could deter after American deterrence had failed. Its reduced vulnerability will tend to make the second-generation deterrent somewhat less dangerous in a crisis by lessening the temptation of an insane pre-emptive strike; but like the first-generation deterrent, it could be used only against cities and could therefore add nothing to the Atlantic deterrent, whose countercity capability is already more than sufficient. Whatever efficacy it does have will depend on the French Government's ability to persuade potential aggressors of its obstinate independence and its absolute refusal to submit to the discipline of a graduated strategy as advocated by the United States. Thus once again French countercity capability will be a functioning deterrent only to the extent to which French leaders manage to appear resolute to the point of blind irrationality in the eyes of their enemies and liable to answer even minor aggression by reprisals serious to the enemy and fatal to France.

This, however, does not mean that even from the viewpoint of security the French decision is indefensible *in the long run.* What would be indefensible is the delusion that in ten years France will no longer need American protection; or any move that, under the guise of strengthening security, would in fact weaken it by goading the United States into retrenching its European commitments. If this can be averted, the ownership of a few dozen bombs and three submarines may constitute some gain for France in the deterrence phase while adding to the risk factor in actual use. A different allocation of these same credits so as to strengthen the bonds between Europe and the United States while giving France more of a voice in the formulation of Atlantic strategy would, in my opinion, yield a greater return (once again, in terms of security only). But the nature of modern arms being what it is, today's decisions may yet prove justified fifteen or twenty years hence. The French force may someday form the nucleus of a European deterrent; in any event it has persuaded our ally, the United States, to enter upon a dialogue with Europe on the subject of strategy. It constitutes an incipient protection against the unpredictability of future diplomacy. The French decision remains a subject for discussion so long as we confine ourselves to the coming decade and regard it as a sort of premium paid now for insurance against an unknown future. Downright absurd, however, is the attempt to transform this project into a symbol of patriotic pride that in ten years' time will replace the American deterrent, consolidate the balance of terror, and at the same time enhance our national self-esteem.

The problems of the French deterrent as it will shape up some ten years from now have nothing whatsoever in common with the ideas of General Gallois, to which we have already had occasion to refer. Although the American press, including some responsible newspapers, has dubbed him the "architect of the striking force" or the adviser to General de Gaulle, the theories of one general should not be confounded with the personal opinions of the other. General de Gaulle in his press conferences has never dealt with atomic strategy in any meaningful detail but has merely confined himself to certain broad statements: "Furthermore, a quality of the atomic force is that it has a certain efficacy, and this to a frightening degree, even where it does not approach the maximum conceivable. . . . I only want to say that the French atomic force will have the somber and terrifying capability of destroying within a few moments millions and millions of people. This cannot help but exert at least some influence upon the intentions of a potential aggressor." These phrases point up what General Gallois refers to as the equalizing power of the atom; they also happen to be platitudes of the first order. No one would want to deny that an "old-fashioned" obsolete Hiroshima-type bomb is still powerful enough to kill thousands of people (always provided the delivery vehicles first penetrate defenses); the notion that under certain conditions a small force may exert a measure of deterrence is not a highly original one.

But beyond such generalities intended to document, as it were, the potential usefulness of a small deterrent, General de Gaulle has never come up with any more detailed theoretical ideas concerning the French atomic effort. He has never expressed misgivings about nuclear proliferation and has refused to commit himself on the subject of nuclear arms for Germany. He has let some of his spokesmen refer to a European deterrent without either disavowing or supporting them.

Not so General Gallois, who, in numerous articles of varying length and style, has indefatigably belabored the notions that were current in U. S. Air Force circles some ten years ago, arranging them in a rigid system of his own—comparable in many ways to the Maginot line. This makes it especially seductive to minds given to oversimplification and pseudo-rationality that at the same time refuse to face the complex facts of reality and the ambiguities of an unknown universe.

General Gallois is a brilliant talker, impassioned, unable so much as to *see* a side other than his own to any question, a mixture of profound inner insecurity and a great show of outward self-assurance that makes him believe that the only conceivable reason for disagreeing with his opinions is stupidity or corruption— "either they are idiots or else they've been bought with U. S. dollars"[16]—an almost perfect example of logic run amuck. Every one of his ideas contains a germ of truth and, within limits, merits attention; but invariably he carries it to a point beyond all plausibility and blows it up into a fish story or a science-fiction tale. Perhaps the mysterious equalizing power of the atom that levels all differences between Switzerland, Monaco, and China also tends to blur the line between reason and lunacy.

Reduced to its simplest terms, Gallois' theory involves two propositions: *atomic power (a) insures peace and (b) dissolves alliances.* He sets out to demonstrate the first proposition by stressing the invulnerability of the deterrents now possessed by the Big Two. The destruction of enemy missile sites requires so many missiles that neither duelist has or ever will have the numerical superiority indispensable to the conduct of an efficient counterforce strategy. The Soviet Union may be able to eliminate the British de-

---

[16] I had the pleasure of writing the preface to his first book, at a time when he did not yet cloak ideas open to debate in extremist formulations and a tone of aggressive chauvinism.

terrent, but the margin of risk of potential failure is sufficiently large to discourage the attempt. The damage that small forces like the French deterrent can inflict will obviously be smaller in scope than that inflicted by a big power upon a small one; but what is at stake is also correspondingly smaller. Thus France, a limited objective, would hardly warrant a big power's risking the destruction of a few cities. This particular proposition led a French admiral, a disciple of the master, to deduce, with a logic worthy of the Mad Hatter, that Denmark could deter the Soviet Union merely by acquiring one nuclear submarine. (It never occurred to the honorable admiral that the Soviet Union might order its submarine chasers to destroy that Danish submarine.)

The first half of the proposition is peace through the atom—the Big Two offsetting each other by the approximate parity of their reciprocal destructive power, the small powers offsetting the big because inequality in the expectation of possible gains makes up for the inequality of destructive power. The second half of the proposition is the obsolescence of alliances. The price of a thermonuclear war, so the argument runs, is so horrendous that no country can afford to take the risk unless its own vital interests are directly involved. Who could possibly believe that the President of the United States would sacrifice Boston or New York in order to save London or Paris? Each nation can count only on itself and no one else; nuclear proliferation, therefore, is not only inevitable but also desirable.

These two basic theses, which Gallois regards as complementary, are in fact largely contradictory, mu-

tually exclusive except insofar as they involve two implicit and implausible assumptions: that the threat of
American retaliation is devoid of *any credibility* so
long as the attack does not directly involve the mainland of the United States, and that a nation with any
kind of atomic force whatsoever is *bound* to strike back
regardless of cost. (If, by way of warning, a big power
destroys half or two thirds of a small power's deterrent, would that country prefer total annihilation to
surrender?)

The conceptual superstructure is no better than the
foundations. It is simply not true that henceforth the
Soviet Union can be *certain* of impunity, provided
only it does not directly attack the mainland of the
United States, any more than it could be *certain* of
instant retaliation if it attacked France armed with
her Mirage IV bombers. The question of whose finger
is on the trigger certainly affects credibility; but to
conclude that it is the *only factor* of importance is
either plain nonsense or else an attempt to exploit the
gullibility of an uninformed public.

We might add at once that this theory is thoroughly
unsuited to the demands of French policy as conducted by General de Gaulle. According to Gallois,
nuclear weapons open the way for most countries to
keep aloof, somewhat in the manner of the neutral
powers of the past; that is, they provide the means
to convince a potential aggressor that the attack would
cost him more than it was worth. This scheme of a
neutrality based on the threat of retaliation is not in
itself contradictory; it is quite possible that in a more
or less distant future some nations will stay out of international conflicts much as Switzerland or Sweden

have in the past, relying on their retaliatory capability as others once relied on forts, mountains, or armies to safeguard their neutrality. But French spokesmen hail the French deterrent as a European force and contrast it with the Anglo-American monopoly; and yet, if the immense power of the United States cannot be expected to protect Europe, how will France manage to protect Berlin or West Germany? Deterrence, if we are to believe the crusading champions of the French national force, applies only to the country actually in possession of the requisite weapons. In that case, who will prevent the Soviet Union from attacking Berlin, Belgium, or Norway? Does every country have to acquire its own bombs, or could the European continent act as a unit?

Let us examine the Gallois theory in some detail. According to him, the value of the American deterrent henceforth is doubtful at best.[17] Imputing his own ideas to the American leaders, he then proceeds to attack the McNamara doctrine, which certainly is open to *valid* criticism, as a web of sneaky and underhanded tricks designed to conceal from the allies the true state of affairs. "As a matter of fact," he writes, "the United States Government has for the past two years been forced to conduct a foreign policy which it can justify to its allies only by a series of contradictory statements, denials, calculated omissions, that is, anti-truths, to put it mildly."[18] It would be hard to conceive of a more

[17] He does not confine himself to stating that vulnerability of the U. S. mainland weakens deterrence, which would have been perfectly acceptable.

[18] From an article in *Nouveau Candide*, Dec. 27, 1962, entitled "Kennedy Is Trying to Trap de Gaulle."

deliberate and more cynical distortion of the United States' approach to the subject.

McNamara and his advisers are at the moment certain of vast U. S. superiority. They therefore, rightly or wrongly, entertain no doubts about the ability of the U. S. deterrent to guarantee the safety of Europe, and are still convinced that the United States retains a substantial strategic counterforce capability, whose progressive decline is to be anticipated, although at a rate increasingly hard to determine.

The new strategy of graduated response is designed to minimize the risk of total war; this does not mean, however, that it is less effective than massive retaliation in deterring limited attacks. In any event, one cannot have it both ways. Either one can object that the strategy of gradual response increases the risks of limited aggression, in which case one cannot deny the present efficacy of the American deterrent in relation to a massive attack, or one can rule out the hypothesis of limited aggression in Europe, in which case, because of the increase of conventional weapons and the several steps of retaliation, American strategy may be futile but it cannot be dangerous, since it is designed for improbable eventualities. Gallois, bent on seeking targets, scatters his shots and quite indiscriminately switches from one position to another without even seeming aware of the inherent contradictions. For instance, in an article that appeared in the review *Politique Etrangère* (No. 5, 1962) he asserts that "there obviously is very little reason to fear an all-out attack, which is the least likely of all possibilities. The danger is not a broad assault on the entire area covered by NATO so much as pressure directed against a sin-

gle member country, in which case the others might
regard the threat as minor, however major it would
seem to the country concerned, and consequently decide to abandon an ally rather than run the formidable
risk of battle."[19]

Let us take his example of a minor attack against
one member of the alliance. The possibility, within
the present context of the total situation, is rather remote; but preventive measures would consist of precisely the suggestions so vehemently rejected by Gallois—reinforcing the links between the individual
members and strengthening interallied solidarity. The
principle of "all for one and one for all" makes "pressure"[20] against one member country inconceivable in
the long run. Quite apart from this objection, however,
a note two pages farther on informs us that "the Soviets
make no mystery of their strategy against Europe.
Khrushchev and Marshal Malinovsky keep repeating
that they would start using their thermonuclear arsenal
in the event of a conflict in Europe. . . . The proponents of a traditional Western strategy ought to
familiarize themselves with Soviet military thinking."
Gallois, on the other hand, ought to reread his own
article and make up his mind which of his propositions he wants to defend. If "there is obviously very little reason to fear an all-out attack," then the statements of Khrushchev and Malinovsky need not be
taken at face value; if, on the other hand, they reflect
Soviet intentions, there is no need to worry about "local
pressure." A polemicist so desperately eager to score

[19] P. 457–58.
[20] Note the vague term used; does pressure mean a diplomatic
threat or aggression with conventional arms?

points that he will shift his grounds in the middle of an argument is liable to trip over his contradictions.[21]

What the experts mainly object to in the McNamara doctrine is that it discriminates between the American mainland, regarded as a sanctuary, and the territory of allied countries. If the sanctuary is attacked, the response will be total; if the allies are attacked, the response will be graduated and may initially be conventional. It is unquestionably true that the McNamara doctrine differentiates between the United States and its allies and that it was born of a desire to minimize the danger of all-out war fought with missile-borne thermonuclear warheads. The crux of the question, however, is whether this new strategy further undermines the security of America's European allies, already shaken by the vulnerability of the United States itself. The charge of discrimination between Europe, covered by the threat of graduated response, and the mainland of the United States, protected by total response, is not entirely fair in that American strategists, even after the start of nuclear exchanges, intend to hold intermediate positions and avoid instant escalation to a thermonuclear spasm (the old massive retaliation concept); but whatever validity it has must be blamed once again on the facts of geography. The United States, separated by several thousand miles from a potential aggressor, cannot be

[21] Contradictions enlisted in the cause of the argument. The strategy of graduated response *may* in effect, under certain circumstances, increase the danger of limited operations. Hence we need not worry about an all-out attack. If, on the other hand, we fear an all-out attack, reinforcement of conventional forces makes no sense. Hence we must fear an all-out attack. The logician scorns logic.

subject to "minor" or "local" aggression. Continental
Europe, on the other hand, borders directly on the
Soviet bloc, and this is the reason that strategists must
plan for a range of contingencies. Even in the era of
conventional arms it was geography rather than the
sinister designs of a McNamara that made the United
States a "sanctuary" and "arsenal of democracy." Up
to the present these facts have not been changed by
the atom.

I am convinced that if France or continental Europe
were to acquire atomic or thermonuclear arms tomorrow, a school of analysts attacking the theory of massive retaliation would immediately arise. They would
stress the dangers of getting trapped in an all-or-nothing situation and point out that, with both sides in
possession of invulnerable deterrents, each threat
would elicit a comparable counterthreat. Would the
enemy in such circumstances let himself be deterred
from limited aggression by an apocalyptic threat that
he has every reason to regard as an empty bluff? In
other words, any country contiguous to a potential aggressor will have to provide for a series of contingencies even if it does possess nuclear arms, unless it has
all by itself, the ability to wipe out the adversary's
retaliatory force. If crime and punishment are approximately equal, the atomic threshold will inevitably be
raised for both opponents because of the wholly incommensurate cost of a thermonuclear war. The more
General Gallois stresses the monstrous horrors of such
a war, the less he has the right to believe that the
threat of one will deter any aggression, regardless of
type or circumstances, just so long as the defender

himself controls the trigger. A nation's threat of suicide becomes persuasive only when its very existence is at stake; within an atomically armed nation the distinction between sanctuaries and non-privileged areas will arise all over again.

Some of General Gallois' objections to the McNamara doctrine are to the point. He stresses the contradiction between the American desire for a strategic counterforce capability and the advice to the Russians to harden their missiles,[22] he justly notes that the "United States does not want to be automatically dragged into a nuclear war because of Europe," and like all other critics he recognizes the risk inherent in the McNamara doctrine:

As long as a potential aggressor is convinced that he cannot unleash aggression without facing the alternatives of surrender or all-out war (i.e., conflict between the United States and the Soviet Union) he is forced to stick to bargaining techniques. But once he has it spelled out that by acquiring conventional as well as nuclear arms he can, without extra risk, obtain a broad margin within which to maneuver, he will be tempted to use force, always provided, of course, that he remains this side of the atomic threshold. In the past this threshold was relatively low, so that, because of the risk of escalation, nuclear deterrence applied at the very first sign of hostility. But if the views of the Kennedy Administration are put into practice and the first rungs of the escalation ladder eliminated —meaning the withdrawal of tactical nuclear weapons from Western Europe—and if nuclear deterrence applies only to the protection of the continental

[22] Though he neglects to explain the reasons that made the Americans hesitate between the contradictory objectives of a strategic counterforce capability on the one hand and an invulnerable Soviet force on the other.

United States, the Soviets will have been put on notice that they can with impunity resort to force in
Europe.

The parenthetical insinuation concerning withdrawal
of tactical nuclear weapons is gratuitous; but in all
other respects these lines rather accurately reflect the
valid objections that Europeans have either raised or
been tempted to raise against the McNamara doctrine: multiplying the intermediary steps between passivity and nuclear war and taking all possible precautions against escalation may in fact increase the danger
of limited wars by persuading the aggressor that he
has a broad area within which to operate without triggering nuclear retaliation.

But General Gallois himself weakens or even altogether refutes this traditional objection by the arguments he uses elsewhere. If the threat of nuclear war
is never credible except where it involves a country's
survival, a U. S. threat of total response would scarcely
be more credible just because some strategists are
committed on paper to the doctrine of massive retaliation. Furthermore, the general keeps insisting that
what he calls "spiralization" (escalation) is inevitable
in Europe. "It is inconceivable," he writes, "that conventional Communist forces would be committed with
any expectation short of conquest, whether by increasing these conventional forces, or by the use of new
types of weapons; spiralization, therefore, is inevitable in Europe."[23] Reinforcement of NATO armies in

[23] *Revue de Défense Nationale*, June 1962. Another point
brought up to bolster this particular argument is the continuity
of power from strongest conventional to weakest tactical nuclear
weapon, which fails to prove that people will not continue to be

such circumstances may prove pointless but can hardly be considered dangerous. If escalation is accepted as inevitable because of Soviet intentions, Soviet leaders in turn must accept its fatal necessity and will henceforth pay scant attention to the subtleties of graduated response, convinced as they are that escalation will have to run its full course.

The same argument could also be formulated in another dilemma. Either the Soviets think they can gain certain objectives by limited use of force without triggering nuclear exchanges—in which case the best way to disabuse them would be to acquire the means needed to stop such aggression without having to resort to nuclear weapons—or they really mean what they say and do not believe in any such distinctions—in which case nothing has been lost. The strategy of graduated response may be futile but would entail no detrimental consequences, since only all-out war will then be possible in Europe.

This objection would carry some weight only if formulated in the following terms: The Russians do not believe in these distinctions and are right not to do so; but merely by insisting often enough on their feasibility one might tempt them into putting the American doctrine to the test, i.e., induce them to engage in limited operations that in fact would be bound to lead to ultimate escalation. Thus an illusory trust in distinctions that have no basis in fact may increase the probability of both minor local aggression calling for

---

aware of the difference between these two types of explosives. What it does in fact prove is that the use of tactical nuclear weapons for defense ought not to be *excluded*—not that it is inevitable.

THE INDEPENDENT FRENCH DETERRENT 133

conventional response and the escalation that the plan seeks above all to avoid.

Given the nature of deterrence, any strategy involves risks. The measure designed to meet one kind of danger will increase another. No one can accurately gauge the probability of various future contingencies; but I personally believe that the strategy of graduated response[24] is best suited to both deterrence and use, always provided that those formulating it publicly (for better or for worse, the discussion of strategy is no longer the exclusive preserve of a small group of experts) make sure they put themselves in a position to practice what they preach. If they do this, and only if they do this, the strategy of graduated response will reduce the element of bluff implicit in all thermonuclear deterrence and will be understood not as an expression of fear or hesitation but as proof of rational resolve.

The major flaw of the McNamara doctrine, according to General Gallois, is the distinction it makes between sanctuaries and open territories; for this he blames the Americans rather than the facts of geography. It follows, inevitably, that "nations possessing a nuclear arsenal will turn their territory into sanctuaries to be defended by the threat of resorting to the ultimate weapons, regardless of consequences and regardless of how credible a threat implying the annihilation of both victim and aggressor may be."[25] This statement illustrates the fallacy at the heart of the general's whole argument. Every country tends to turn it-

---

[24] Which does not mean that the idea of using tactical nuclear arms is ruled out; quite the contrary.

[25] *Revue de Défense Nationale*, June 1962, p. 951.

self into a sanctuary the moment it acquires a "nuclear
arsenal" for its own purposes. General Gallois' thinking, shaped during the period of unilateral deterrence
in U. S. Air Force circles, has remained stuck at the
level of massive retaliation in its crudest form. Each
nation, as it acquires nuclear weapons, will in turn
adopt this doctrine as its own. A moment's reflection
will, however, reveal the utter absurdity of spreading
the theory of massive retaliation.

The confrontation of two relatively small countries,
both armed with nuclear weapons, would make for
extreme instability unless neither could hope to destroy the enemy's means of retaliation by a pre-emptive strike; otherwise the advantages of aggression
become as disproportionately large as the extent of destruction inflicted on the first-strike victim. The theory,
therefore, applies only if all nuclear forces are relatively invulnerable, a condition difficult to meet within
the foreseeable future and certainly not obtaining for
the Mirage IV bombers.

But even if this obstacle were overcome, would possession of a small deterrent really enable a country to
proclaim itself an inviolate sanctuary simply by threatening, regardless of circumstances, to take the step
that would mean self-destruction? How credible is
such a threat?[26] The United States never applied the
doctrine of massive retaliation even when its own territory was still invulnerable; it is even less applicable
to relations among countries that all have *more or less
invulnerable nuclear forces.* If every country with a
small nuclear arsenal were to be guided by this doc-

[26] General Gallois intimates that the credibility is not altogether certain.

trine, the risk of explosion would accrue with each new member's joining the atomic club. No country can afford to concentrate all its resources on nuclear arms exclusively unless it is part of an alliance; and none can afford to brandish the threat of nuclear reprisals in any and all circumstances. It was the Atlantic Alliance that in the years past enabled France to commit the bulk of her forces abroad and that, in the years to come, may make it possible for her to reduce conventional forces in favor of the atomic program.

When it comes to confrontations between big and small powers, General Gallois believes that the unequal danger they face is theoretically offset by the trivial nature of any possible gains that a big power stands to obtain by victory.

Here again the idea is not wholly devoid of truth. Given the power of thermonuclear arms, a nation does not have to match the enemy in a one-to-one relationship of weapons and missiles in order to reach a state of balance; within certain limits the concept of minimum deterrence is valid. A nation with an invulnerable reprisal force of several dozen missiles fitted with thermonuclear warheads could deter a far more powerful country from direct aggression. But if retaliatory capability beyond a certain point may deter an enemy from *some types* of attack, it still will not deter him from any and all aggression. The aggressor would abstain from action liable to trip off nuclear retaliation, but the defender in turn is not going to unleash it except in extreme circumstances; he cannot legitimately invoke the apocalyptic character of nuclear war and at the same time rely on the "credibility" of his nuclear threat.

A nation regarded as small, such as France, could deter the Soviet Union from direct aggression if it had a minimal retaliatory capability of perhaps a few dozen missiles sure to survive an attack and able to strike back at major targets in enemy territory. There is no need even to stress the discrepancy between necessary force and expectation of gain in order to prove that in the nuclear age a small power can sometimes defy a big one. But neither the first- nor the second-generation French deterrent will reach this level of efficacy, and there is no assurance that the third-generation one will do so, given the imponderables of the scientific and technological progress that the major powers will make in the meantime. No ally of the United States will be able to meet the conditions of potential balance between big and small powers by an independent effort in the next twenty years. Britain might have the best chance, but she is relying on the U. S. radar network and is half committed not to act on her own. The fact remains that France will not be able to deter attacks against her until 1975 at the earliest and will derive no added protection from her own atomic force while her future is at stake in Berlin or in the Federal Republic. In the context of present international relations, whatever slight deterrence France can exert in the coming ten to fifteen years will bolster her security only to the extent that if American commitment continues unchanged, the French force will add another element of uncertainty to the combination facing Soviet strategists.

Going beyond the present context, however, let us imagine France or Switzerland, or for that matter Monaco, alone and unassisted facing the Soviet Union.

Would the equalizing power of the atom, combined
with the proportionality of deterrence, miraculously
level the difference between dwarf and giant? The
conditions as stipulated by General Gallois are as follows: the bulk[27] of Soviet resources is concentrated in
some sixty urban clusters; any small power able to
destroy all, three quarters, or even half of them on
second strike wields a threat whose deadly effects
would far outweigh any advantages the big power
could possibly hope to gain by conquest (even if
France were to be the potential prize). True enough;
but to deduce from this that Switzerland or Monaco
may ultimately be able to acquire the second-strike
capability needed to destroy some dozens of Soviet
cities is pure casuistry. This type of speculative
thought may serve a purpose by providing an abstract
model of one possibility inherent in the atomic universe; but as a guiding principle justifying actual policy decisions, it recalls Khrushchev's favorite proverb
about the whistling shrimps.

Even within the framework of this abstraction it is
by no means accurate to suggest either that nuclear
weapons have abolished space or that their efficient
use requires vast territorial expanses. Both General
Gallois at one extreme and Jules Moch at the other
misinterpret one aspect of the problem. While it is
true that urban concentration tends to reduce the advantage of a large territory as soon as the means of
delivery have attained a sufficient degree of accuracy,
a few dozen bombs hitting a small and densely populated country can wipe out the whole nation. A theo-

[27] 90 per cent of the intellectual potential, 70 per cent of the
economic potential, 60 per cent of the demographic potential.

rist may postulate that beyond a certain point of devastation all distinctions between more and less cease
to be meaningful; and people may, of course—though
even here I am not sure—come to feel that there is no
real difference between losing one third, two thirds or
the entire population. But this attitude would influence the conduct of the small power as much as it
would that of the big, with the latter at least not being
trapped in a choice between all or nothing, massive
aggression or passivity. The small power (endowed
here for argument's sake with a retaliatory capability)
would have to decide whether to take the initiative of
escalation regardless of diplomatic pressure and of the
scope of a conventional attack. If a big power carried
out a military operation and within hours seized the
objective in dispute, would the small power respond
by a nuclear strike? What government, of what small
nation, would have the courage or the foolhardiness
to choose extermination rather than surrender when
faced with the choice?

I want to make clear that I am not disputing that
any country, once it acquires a retaliatory capability
(relatively invulnerable forces) can exert some degree
of deterrence even vis-à-vis a major power; what I
deny is that in a test of nerves the leaders of a country
risking total annihilation are the equals of those whose
country would merely sustain some losses. I do not
agree that differences in the ability to absorb punishment—largely a function of territorial size—have
ceased to be meaningful, nor do I agree that a small
power can deter any type of aggression by the threat
of massive retaliation. Neither the value of a given objective nor the degree of risk which this value would

logically justify an aggressor to take can, in my opinion, be computed with absolute precision. The scope and significance of a confrontation between two powers armed with nuclear weapons in itself far transcends the material objectives at stake in any crisis, as was clearly evident during the Cuban crisis. If a big power, by using its thermonuclear superiority, managed to bludgeon into acquiescence or surrender another country equipped with a smaller nuclear arsenal, the terror inspired everywhere would constitute a gain far transcending the mere conquest of territory or material resources.

General Gallois exaggerates beyond all reason the efficacy of the threat wielded by a small country equipped with nuclear arms; with the same deficient sense of proportion he attempts to disparage the American deterrent, going so far as to misquote others for this purpose.[28] In the final analysis, what is the point of saying that the United States will not sacrifice New York and Boston for London and Paris, or that Americans cannot be expected to pull the trigger if this would cost them millions of dead? All these statements begin by assuming the failure of deterrence, and then proceed to speculate on what the Americans would do in such a case. Exactly the same line of reasoning, however, can with equal ease prove the futility of

[28] In an article in the *Nouveau Candide* he did not mention one of the three situations in which, according to General Taylor, the U. S. ought to resort to nuclear arms: direct attack on the United States, imminence of direct attack, and massive attack on Western Europe. General Gallois, thoroughly familiar with the text since he quotes it elsewhere, chose to omit the third hypothesis in his article, entitled "Kennedy Is Trying to Trap de Gaulle" (the title may have been the editor's contribution).

national deterrents. If half of France had been destroyed in an initial assault, would the President of the Republic still issue orders for an absurd retaliatory strike in full awareness that it would imply total destruction of what was left of the country? The uncertainty of the response is part of the strategy of deterrence. Obviously no one can tell what would transpire in the mind of the man occupying the White House if Soviet tanks were to roll into West Berlin or large formations of Soviet troops crossed the line of demarcation in Europe. Deterrence is based on risk rather than certainty. But by keeping half a million of its citizens in Europe, two thirds of them in uniform, and by using every possible opportunity to reaffirm its ties with the destiny of Western Europe and its determination to defend the freedom of West Berlin, the United States has made its commitment as complete and solemn as possible. Khrushchev himself has never had any doubts on this score, even if in private conversations he has professed to regard it as a bluff, at least where West Berlin is concerned. He has never gone so far as to try and call the bluff, to see if the United States would honor its promise. Deterrence has worked.

General Gallois, describing the "spiral" (escalation) that according to him is inevitable, at least in Europe, refuses to acknowledge any discontinuity between the first and last rungs of the ladder of violence; to him the only real commitment is that in which anyone possessing a nuclear capability uses and abuses the threat of total retaliation. There is no place in his "logic of the atomic age" for common-sense axioms, such as that a big power may protect areas other than its own

whose territorial integrity it considers vital by so notifying its rival, and that major powers have always
respected each other's vital interests so long as they
wanted to avoid a struggle unto death. Once upon a
time dogma had it that the Maginot line was impreg-
nable; dogma now has it that *any and all* countries in
possession of a nuclear arsenal—and they *alone*—can
set themselves up as self-sufficient sanctuaries.

Obviously only those benighted minds who obsti-
nately resist the idea that the atomic age has abolished
all differences between a part and the whole, between
a major disaster and a total catastrophe, between in-
jury and death, between tragic losses and extermination, could possibly persist in the belief that Khrushchev might be deterred more effectively by the
immense power of the United States, even when acting on behalf of France, than by the Mirage IV
bombers.

General Gallois is neither the ideologist of the
French deterrent nor the spokesman for General de
Gaulle, and fortunately, a rational interpretation of the
French atomic program does not hinge on this sort of
specious reasoning. It is enough to salvage the frag-
ment of truth that Gallois stretches to absurdity.
France did not want to be excluded from nuclear technology. She did not want the entire continent to be
permanently dependent solely on the protection of the
Anglo-Americans. She took a more or less long-range
view of world affairs that included possible realign-
ments in international constellations. She was taking
out insurance against the unforeseen and the unforeseeable. And furthermore, any deterrent, no matter

how limited, adds impact to her diplomatic moves and increases her chance to influence the strategy of the ally responsible for the essential deterrence. Even if it seems hard to believe that the threat to use the French deterrent as a detonator could influence Soviet leaders, these questions relate more to psychology than to logic; and there is no denying that the French deterrent adds yet another factor to those the Soviet high command, presumed eager to launch an aggression, must take into account.[29] Coming back now to the four types of return enumerated at the beginning of this chapter, let us say in conclusion that the low security return over the next ten years demolishes most

---

[29] Professor Stanley Hoffmann of Harvard, a more subtle proponent of the French deterrent than its official spokesmen, "proves" the "deterrence" value of the French force as follows: "In case of extreme Soviet provocation against Western Europe, the French threat of a thermonuclear strike (a threat that the Americans regard themselves as less and less able to brandish except in the most serious circumstances) and the counterthreat of annihilating France, which the Russians will not hesitate to make in return, would force the U. S. into a manifestation of its solidarity with France—or in other words extend the cover of its nuclear protection to France even if this was precisely the sort of situation it had wanted to avoid. Strategic dissent and France's 'disobedience' would not, after all, be sufficient reason to justify abandoning France, the less so since abandoning France to Russian bombs would be a disaster for the United States as well. The manifest purpose, then, is preventive triggering designed to *deter* the Russians ahead of time rather than countering an attack after the fact." The flaw in this argument is that if the Americans don't want to go to extremes, they have ample means to make known their refusal. Furthermore, it is hard to see how France could make this move for the sake of "Western Europe," i.e., risk devastation in order to protect Berlin, Western Germany or Norway. As long as we are toying with hypotheses, it would be safer to assume only that the Russians cannot take it for granted that the French would not do so. The threat, though not explicit, of using the French atomic force as detonator is its sole conceivable deterrent function within the framework of the present Atlantic organization.

of the official arguments. But the program is better than its proponents, and France would be able to justify it if she spoke and acted as behooves a big power. This, in our day, means showing awareness of the problems that these weapons, whose ultimate function is to prevent their own use, have created for alliances as well as for mankind as a whole.

5

The Future of the Atlantic Alliance

War offices and general staff headquarters in pre-atomic days collected filing cabinets full of operational plans, all designed to meet any of the various contingencies that the fertile brains of diplomats or soldiers were capable of dreaming up. But these plans, classified "Top Secret" and carefully protected at least from the prying curiosity of common mortals if not always of enemy spies, were not subject to public discussion and could not possibly cause friction among allies—especially since allies almost never went so far as to agree on a joint course of action in advance of the outbreak of hostilities.

But, as Molière's "physician in spite of himself" put it, "we've changed all that." Any journalist, politician or diplomat now feels qualified to hold forth on the respective merits of counterforce versus countercity strategy or on the deployment of tactical atomic weapons. American refusal to install medium-range missiles on European soil becomes a topic for polemics. Measures, even mere suggestions, of a purely military nature are interpreted as symptoms of political intentions. Ever since 1961, when the Kennedy Administration took over in Washington, atomic and thermonuclear arms have become the central issue in controversies among the Western allies on the one hand and between China and the Soviet Union on the other.

In the old days every government relied on the interval that normally followed the rupture of diplomatic relations but preceded the actual outbreak of war. Surprises, of course, were not wholly unknown; history records any number of times when sovereign territory was invaded without prior warning. Twice the Japanese sank enemy fleets—first the Russian, then the American—whose admirals were unaware that hostilities had already begun. But even in these exceptional cases, where no due and formal declaration of war preceded sudden aggression, the victims were not permanently put out of commission; they had reserves to fall back on and time to mobilize them. The explosive power of nuclear weapons and the speed of delivery, however, are such that henceforth no major power can afford to shirk the obligation of a permanent alert. It is doubtful whether the mobilization of human and industrial resources is still feasible in the wake of nuclear exchanges, and at least in the event of all-out war there will be no discernible difference between the forces available in peacetime and those that can be mobilized in time of war.[1]

---

[1] By way of another paradox, mobilization in the traditional manner will now take place only for secondary conflicts of the

Permanent mobilization is part of the permanent alert; and the measures taken—deployment of divisions and of tactical atomic weapons—predetermine the course of events.

Since the prime objective of these measures is deterrence—that is, the prevention of hostilities—strategy and diplomacy are now intertwined as never before. At every step along the way, before the start as well as during the course of hostilities, politics or, to use Clausewitz's phrase, the intelligence of the state, must remain in full charge of an action that combines word and deed and in which the deed, potential or actual, is only a proposition and appeal to reason addressed to the enemy. Words alone are wasted unless they convey a threat backed up by military measures.

This situation, inevitable though it may be, entails obvious risks. In the old days staff headquarters did not regard certain contingencies as likely simply because they had provided for them in their advance planning. Today one is sometimes inclined to feel that the West fears certain dangers not because they are real but because planners have included them in order not to omit any theoretically conceivable Soviet move. It is almost as if the less cause there is to fear Soviet aggression, the more the West worries about it. The arguments have grown more intense not because people are increasingly sophisticated and can now perceive situations that ten years ago, when nations were less well armed and less well informed, would have escaped their attention. What scares them, in a way,

Korean type or to demonstrate "resolve" as a means of deterrence, as for instance in the Berlin crisis of 1961.

is their own shadow; and the American analysts are scaring Europeans by taking precautions against contingencies that to the latter seem improbable, to say the least.

I deliberately stopped at the year 1957 in my analysis of the influence of atomic weapons on international relations. Before going on to the contemporary phase I wanted to examine the evolution of American strategic theory, the McNamara doctrine and the European reactions to it. Since 1958 and 1959, atomic weapons have transformed relations among allies as much as among enemies and have shaken both power blocs in such a way as to create a more favorable climate for an incipient détente between enemies. The damage to European security as a result of the increasing vulnerability of the United States has never been evident except in books and newspapers; it was felt far more acutely by specialists, statesmen and experts than by the man in the street.

Here again the paradox is apparent rather than real. In theory the experts are right: the threat of thermonuclear arms becomes more and more implausible as the possibilities of devastation to which anyone resorting to it would expose himself increase. But the devastation would be no less terrible for the nation provoking this outburst of insanity, so that extreme provocation is no more probable than the thermonuclear response. Thus the two major powers have, by gradually feeling their way, come to discover and respect certain simple rules. Neither has pushed the use of thermonuclear arms to extremes in diplomatic offensives, and neither has taken the military initiative in a zone of influence staked out by the other, at least where a line of demarcation had clearly been traced.[2]

These rules—to refrain from using regular armies to modify the status quo and from using the thermonuclear threat to obtain concessions—conform to the extreme prudence dictated by the monstrous destructiveness of the weapons available, but they are also in line with traditional Bolshevik concepts. Obviously the Bolsheviks are not loathe to spread socialism at the point of the bayonet, as they proved in 1921 against those provinces of the Czar's former empire rash enough either to take seriously the·right-of-secession clause in the new Soviet Constitution or else to choose governments with a dissenting ideology. Likewise, when the occasion seemed ripe in 1939–40 and in 1944–45, they did not hesitate to "convert" the populations whose territory the Red Army had occupied or, rather, to comport themselves as armed prophets, with Soviet troops clearing the way for the People's Commissars. But except for the North Korean aggression (which at the very least they condoned), the Soviets under Stalin as well as under Khrushchev have never contemplated waging a major war for the sole purpose of advancing the cause of socialism. The nature of thermonuclear arms is such that even the Soviet premier no longer regards a Third World War as the final and inevitable stage of the present world crisis marking the transition from capitalism to socialism.

Constant and careful thought will from now on have to be devoted to the best ways of meeting any emergency, including raids, local aggression against one

[2] The exception of Cuba will be examined later on.

member of an alliance, aggressive probes, major aggression with conventional arms only, and massive aggression. At the same time, however, it would be quite unreasonable to ascribe to the enemy wholly improbable intentions that are conceived exclusively for the purpose of preventing them.

Whatever the actual deployment of NATO troops and whatever the doctrine officially proclaimed—graduated response or total response—Western Europe as seen from Moscow resembles nothing so much as a powder keg which the least spark is liable to set off. Neither Soviet rules of conduct nor the European situation is likely to lure the Kremlin into testing a strategy of minor aggression that relies on the manifest American reluctance to unleash a total response or to provoke an immediate escalation.

For yet another reason—never, to my knowledge, properly emphasized—the American strategy of graduated response does not, for the time being, seem so likely to increase the probability, or reduce the improbability, of limited operations as is generally believed. The fact is that *up to now Soviet leaders and theoreticians have refused to subscribe to the ingenious distinctions so carefully elaborated by the American analysts.*

This point calls for some reservations. We do not know with any degree of certainty just what strategic doctrine has in fact been adopted either by the Soviet government or by the military leaders. All speeches and books that appear in the Soviet Union, even those of an apparently scientific character, inevitably contain an ideological component, a dash of propaganda. Moreover, the strategy of deterrence can not be conducted without an element of bluff. The Soviet leaders, in their answer to the twenty-five points raised by the Central Committee of the Chinese Communist Party, maintain that they would counter any U. S. aggression against Cuba with thermonuclear missiles. No one can tell whether this claim would be backed up in the hour of truth. Subject to this reservation, however, the fact remains that Soviet theoreticians seem rather baffled by the strategic universe that the American analysts have constructed, and Premier Khrushchev in particular seems definitely opposed to this sort of speculation. If he is to be believed, any conflict involving the two thermonuclear powers would fatally escalate to extremes, i.e., become both global and total.

Let us assume that he really thinks so (a not unlikely assumption) and examine the possible consequences. The Soviet Union seems to act as though it were satisfied with what the American theoreticians refer to as a *minimum deterrent*.[3] It has not mass-produced strategic bombers able to strike at targets located within the continental United States, nor has it produced the hundreds of intercontinental missiles that U. S. experts worried about in 1957–58. Whether because of inadequate resources or because they want to put more effort into succeeding generations of missiles, the Soviets have confined themselves to offsetting the huge American system by a certain response capability (a retaliatory capability that they consider secure regardless of circumstances), and by superiority in intermediate-range missiles over Western Europe's means

[3] Meaning a retaliatory capability sufficient to inflict, in response to any direct aggression, destruction deemed unacceptable to the enemy.

of defense or response.[4] They do not explicitly claim to be able to destroy the American retaliatory force, but they intimate that once nuclear explosives start "speaking," nothing will be able to arrest escalation, and that they themselves will simultaneously attack launching ramps, airports, and cities.

The United States for its part has, or thinks it has and will continue to have for a few more years, a certain strategic counterforce capability. It claims that it is in the common interest of both sides, recognized by both, to attempt to limit a conflict if and when one does break out. American policy, therefore, is to multiply the intermediate steps between total passivity and thermonuclear paroxysm. In American eyes the advocates of massive retaliation seem immoral (the amount of force applied should bear some relation to the significance of the crime committed or object at stake), imprudent (what will they do if backed against a wall?) and foolish (do they not understand that this sort of doctrine is tantamount to a bluff that sooner or later is bound to end in tragedy?).

The Soviet theoreticians, as seen from the perspective of Washington, are irrational. Thermonuclear arms make it necessary to revive, by way of technical innovation, the old doctrine of limited wars. The military leader must attempt to impose his will upon the enemy, but reason compels him to do so at the lowest cost to himself, and sometimes even to his opponent. In the old days one could always regard the destruction of the enemy's armed forces as equivalent to total victory. Nowadays the destruction is liable to involve the

[4] This was the meaning of Khrushchev's remark to a U. S. journalist in 1962 that he was holding Europe hostage.

entire country rather than merely the armed forces, unless the restraint formerly urged upon military leaders in the mobilization of resources and the exploitation of victory is introduced into the conduct of the operations themselves. The American analysts consider that differentiation between the various possible phases, separating minor operations carried out with conventional arms from an all-out thermonuclear paroxysm, is the obvious and inevitable consequence of the technological revolution set off by thermonuclear arms.

The Americans regard the Soviet thesis as all the more irrational in that it keeps the Russians from exploiting their own unquestionable superiority. If we consider the situation in Europe, we find that Europeans no longer regard a massive Soviet attack as a major danger. Such an attack would in all probability provoke a nuclear response from the United States;   in any event it would entail the destruction of Western Europe, the very area for whose possession the aggressor would have taken an incommensurate risk. What Europeans now either fear or pretend to fear is that the subtle sophistry of a graduated response might tempt the Russians into a partial attack held below the atomic threshold. Luckily, however, the Russians, by refusing to believe in the possibility of limiting the scope of a conflict, aid in reducing the dangers created by the American theory.

The present asymmetry between Soviet and American theories is all the more paradoxical in that each country seems to be adopting the doctrine more appropriate to the other's military situation. The Russians have the upper hand in conventional arms at many

points along the borders[5] that separate the two worlds
and hence would stand to gain from propagating the
idea that containment of hostilities is possible; that
thermonuclear arms constitute a "shield," a deterrent
that will prevent the enemy from using his own thermonuclear arms; and that henceforth conventional
arms are the "sword," the weapon of choice when it
comes to dealing with the enemy at a low level of violence, with both sides being protected from escalation
by the monstrous nature of the ultimate weapons.

I have often wondered whether or not it would be
desirable for Soviet leaders to undergo a training period at the Rand Corporation.[6] In a somewhat more
serious vein, one might ask if in the interest of world
peace it would be better for the leaders of both thermonuclear powers to think along analogous or divergent lines. Mutual understanding is imperative among
allies, and the controversies within the Atlantic Alliance derive at least partly from misunderstandings;
but the doctrinal asymmetry between Russians and
Americans and the absence of understanding, or at
least the suspicion with which each side continues to
view the other, may very well favor the prevention of
war, limited or otherwise.

The Americans are in fact familiar with the officially
proclaimed Russian doctrine that denies the possibility
of limiting any conflict between the Big Two. They are

[5] Possibly no longer on the central front in Europe if American intelligence is right.
[6] American analysts to whom I posed this question were reluctant to commit themselves. It would be preferable for Khrushchev to have a more flexible strategy when it comes to reducing the risk of all-out war; but this flexibility might in turn give
him certain advantages.

far from taking the Russians at their word,[7] and in the 1962 Cuban crisis for the first time they successfully tested their own doctrine of the "shield" or "sword." But what they regard as Russian simple-mindedness nonetheless effectively spurs them to an even greater caution; as long as the Russians cling to the primitive strategy of thermonuclear spasm, even if it may merely be so much talk, the Americans consider it the better part of wisdom to avoid direct confrontation at almost any price. The Russians in turn are not unaware of American theories, and their experts probably understand them too. But they must again be thinking somewhat along the lines of "How can you figure those damned Yankees? They tell you that they aren't interested in Korea and then they spend three years fighting for it, and after that they reduce the risk of escalation to a complex verbal construct as though they absolutely wanted to bait us into limited operations below the atomic threshold! What would really happen the day the fate of the world came to depend on such subtleties?"

Thus inadequate understanding coupled with mutual suspicion tends to keep each side from moving against the other. Mutual understanding, with both opponents subscribing to the same doctrine, whether of inevitable escalation or of multiple intermediate steps, might not be preferable at all. Russia and the United States threatening total response on every occasion would be rather like two poker players bluffing all the time or two drivers playing "chicken"; inevitably

[7] As Albert Wohlstetter put it, "Between crises the Russians play poker; but once the crisis comes to a head they too play chess."

the moment is bound to arrive when neither "chickens out." If both sides were to act upon the first doctrine, the results in the long run would be disastrous. But the second doctrine, if perfectly assimilated by the Big Two, would again involve dangers of its own. Each side would believe it safe to wield the "sword"—i.e., superiority in conventional arms wherever this applies —without serious risk of escalation. Once this happens, the two camps could regain security only by a kind of parity at all levels. But deterrence by conventional arms has never been wholly effective in the past and is even less likely to work today if each side, familiar with the other's way of thinking, stops being afraid of escalation.

This paean in praise of strategic asymmetry or lack of understanding is really less of a paradox than it seems. The one type of communication that the analysts regard as absolutely essential is the capacity to communicate at the moment of crisis, a function of the "hot line." Misunderstanding of strategic doctrines in advance of a crisis is a component of that same uncertainty whose necessity (in the dual sense of being both inevitable and indispensable) the analysts have stressed time and again. Of course, this is quite different from the classic concept of uncertainty. If A wants to deter B by making him fear the worst ahead of time and B refuses to let himself be deterred, A retreats before the apocalypse. He does not wish for perfect communications in advance of a crisis, but once it comes to a head, he thinks them desirable in order to avoid being impaled on the horns of a dilemma between surrender or death. The American doctrine aims at reducing the contradiction between strategy of deterrence

and strategy of use implicit in the formula of massive
retaliation; in the long run it is bound to spread, but
stability at the upper level will have to be paid for by
increased instability at the lower one. For the time
being the uncertainty derives from the disparity between the Soviet threat of total response and the
American threat of graduated response, with neither
side fully accepting the other's professed doctrine at
face value.[8]

An odd feature of this duel is that the Americans are
playing chess while the Russians play poker. Now the
Russians are the world's champion chess players, while
the theory of games was worked out in Princeton
around a poker table. Yet the American strategy of
graduated response and calculated moves, of anticipating and weighing the possible countermoves, is closer
to chess while the Soviet strategy of brandishing the
apocalyptic threat and preparing to retreat if blackmail is met with resolve is much more typical of poker.

It is possible that this paradox is explicable if the
Soviet purpose is to eliminate the use of armed forces
altogether and to play chess exclusively, but at a purely
political level—subversion and guerrilla warfare being
considered an integral part of politics.

As I have said, only once did the Soviets break the
unwritten rules on the use of ballistic missiles in dip-

[8] One objection may be raised against this analysis: as long
as the Americans have a certain counterforce capability, the Russians cannot use their conventional superiority as a "sword" because they do not want to give their rivals the advantage of a
first strike. This, in fact, constitutes the rationalization of the
Soviet doctrine according to the American theory. Personally I
am not sure that this rational formulation corresponds to the
authentic motive.

lomatic offenses.[9] Only once did the Big Two directly confront one another, one side taking the initiative by provocatively installing medium-range missiles some 125 miles off the coast of Florida, the other responding by a quasi-ultimatum, demanding and obtaining the withdrawal of Russian missiles, but in exchange for a more or less explicit[10] American promise not to invade the island.

The American strategists who developed the conceptual basis of the policy, or perhaps even directed the operation, saw in it a confirmation of their doctrine. For the first time, in fact, conventional forces served as a "sword" while at a higher level nuclear forces neutralized each other. To put it more simply, the Americans threatened to seize or destroy the Russian missiles unless they were withdrawn, and superiority in conventional arms would have enabled them to take such action without going beyond local hostilities. The Soviets, on the other hand, had no local defensive capability; the choice they faced was either to liquidate the episode as best they could, or to react at another point along the border between the two worlds, or to scale the first rungs of escalation—that is, to use atomic weapons, or at least threaten to do so. The Americans' own conceptual system should have led them to expect the second alternative. In fact, the danger of both camps' being guided by the same doctrine, accepting the nuclear stalemate and using conventional forces as

[9] In the Berlin crisis Khrushchev indicated diplomatically offensive use, but in a much more vague manner. See below, p. 221.
[10] The promise was explicit in exchange for the on-the-spot inspection. Castro opposed inspection, and the promise no longer fully applies.

a "sword," is that each side has numerous opportunities to score over the other. The Soviet Union actually enjoys a decided advantage in this respect because, as a centrally located inland power, it can maneuver along inner lines of communication and, with its larger army and its less demanding population, can in many areas wield a sword more effective than that of its adversary.

However, as we now know, the Soviets without much apparent hesitation decided on the simplest and most prudent reply. They gave in to American pressure without even so much as consulting their protégé, probably out of fear of an American attack that a deliberately unleashed propaganda campaign had made them regard as imminent. Such an attack would have confronted them with a choice between loss of face and escalation. From everything we know about the Soviets, they would have chosen loss of face. But their quick compliance forestalled the American attack; and President Kennedy, in line with a thesis popular among the strategic analysts, attempted to disguise his success and leave his adversary an honorable way out, so that Premier Khrushchev could represent the outcome as a reasonable compromise marked by equivalent concessions on both sides.

The Chinese Party, not without reason, accused its Russian brother of having committed a twofold error: to begin with, "adventurism" on the tactical plane in constructing a missile base off the Florida coast, and "capitulationism" thereafter in the indecent haste of the retreat. Khrushchev, or the Russian Party, officially replied in July 1963 and, in a letter rebutting one by one the twenty-five points raised by the Chinese, asserted that the first step—installation of missiles—was not "adventurism," because its purpose had been to prevent or deter an imminent American invasion, and that the second was not "capitulationism" since the original goal had been accomplished once the Americans were forced to drop their invasion project.

Anyone but an unconditionally dedicated disciple of Moscow will find it hard to swallow this retrospective version. Not a shred of evidence exists that President Kennedy, who had denied air cover to the Cuban exiles in the 1961 Bay of Pigs invasion, had any intention of mounting an invasion in 1962 when Soviet-Cuban defenses in conventional arms, considerably reinforced, could have been overcome only by a much more extensive effort than would have been required two years earlier.

The calculations that went into the Kremlin move remain unknown. Personally, I consider them simply the result of an inaccurate appraisal by the Soviet premier of President Kennedy and of the American people. In 1961 and 1962 Western visitors brought back many pronouncements by Khrushchev on the subject of Westerners in general and President Kennedy in particular; the West, he said, was bluffing and would never fight for Berlin. And how could an old Bolshevik have respected an American President who had neither stopped the Cuban exiles from invading nor yet helped them to victory? If the Marines had intervened in the Bay of Pigs invasion, Khrushchev would have called on the whole world to witness this latest example of cynical imperialist immorality, but at the same time he would have had due respect for his rival. Halfway cynicism, on the other hand, coupled with scruples end-

ing in humiliation in the shame of having ventured and
failed, must have given the old fighter an entirely er-
roneous idea of the young President.

In June 1950 Stalin had not foreseen that Washington, though indifferent to South Korea at the strategic
level, would not countenance open violation of the
United Nations charter, an invasion by a regular army
and the dismemberment of a country created by the
United States within its own zone of occupation. Simi-
larly Khrushchev, in all likelihood, did not expect that
Kennedy, after failing to react to the arrival of Soviet
arms and specialists in Cuba, would not tolerate the
installation of missiles—despite the fact that the President had made this amply clear when he drew a line
between offensive and defensive weapons and publicly
announced that *he would not permit emplacement of
offensive weapons on the island.* The warning failed
to deter Khrushchev and his men from trying, but
Moscow's vague threats of protecting Cuba with rockets equally failed to deter the United States. Instead of
gaining a sudden advantage—psychological even more
than military—by unveiling Soviet missile bases in
Cuba, that he might have been able to exploit in Berlin, Khrushchev, quite to the contrary, found success
and psychological initiative changing sides and passing
to President Kennedy.

To regard the Cuban episode as conclusive confirmation of American theories and doctrines would be to
overstate the case. All circumstances in this instance
combined to favor the Americans. They held an overwhelming local superiority in conventional arms. The
theater of operations was close to their homegrounds
and thousands of miles removed from Russian bases.

The average Soviet citizen knew nothing about the Cuban People's Republic and might have found it rather difficult to understand why he should expose himself to terrifying danger for the sake of so trifling an objective. American public opinion, on the other hand, was at fever pitch and goading the President, who would have jeopardized his political future if by inaction he had countenanced the establishment of Soviet missile base in Cuba. The psychological factor, therefore, was weighted heavily in favor of the United States, since it was superior locally in conventional arms and its stakes in the encounter were infinitely greater than what the Russians could expect to gain.

Finally we must remember that the retreat was an honorable one and that ultimately the American success proved limited in scope. Cuba remains a Soviet military base, powerfully defended against any invasion attempts carried out with only conventional arms as well as a focus of subversion from which propaganda and guerrilla fighters spread throughout Latin America. In material terms the episode, as far as Moscow is concerned, amounted simply to a no-sale transaction; the Russians withdrew only the missiles, while President Kennedy failed to demand—as he probably could have done—the withdrawal of all Soviet military personnel.[11]

In the area of atomic strategy, the Cuban episode

[11] I am not discussing the interpretation according to which Kennedy is supposed to have promised withdrawal of missiles from Turkey and Italy in return; that move had been decided on long before. Nor can I accept the arguments of those indignant over the blockade; would Russia tolerate the installation of missiles in Finland if that country were to join the Western camp?

lends itself to other interpretations as well. Thus, according to Stanley Hoffmann, "the Americans claim, first, that Cuba proved their determination to defend vital U. S. interests and, furthermore, that the crisis demonstrated the advantage of superiority in conventional arms. But in the eyes of many Europeans what the episode really proved was, first, that the peace of the world may continue to be jeopardized by Soviet moves based on inadequate appreciation of American resolve; second, that if the automobile[12] cracks up because the driver failed to signal a turn far enough ahead of time, the passengers will be killed along with the driver; third, that in the Cuban encounter the automobile was able to scare the Soviets off the highway not only because it was more powerful but also because the driver gave visible evidence of his manifest determination not to flinch from escalation if it came to it." These three points are correct but contribute no decisive argument to either side in the great debate that rages within the Atlantic Alliance. It is true that determination to escalate in case of need is essential to the efficacy of either use or the threat of use of conventional arms, but the American strategists have never denied this. The orthodox doctrine postulates *the risk of escalation* but does not conceive of it as *being automatic*. To point out that there must be readiness to escalate if need be implies criticism not of McNamara's advisers, but (at the very most) of spokesmen who

[12] The metaphor stems from a speech by Walter Lippmann delivered on the seventy-fifth anniversary of the Paris edition of the New York *Herald Tribune*, who likened the Atlantic Alliance to an automobile. The passengers, i.e., the Allies, may argue about the route ahead of time, but ultimately they must trust the driver, i.e., the United States.

confine themselves to promoting a single aspect of the doctrine—the effort to avoid escalation—rather than stressing equally the threat of escalation along with the simultaneous effort to avert it.

It is unquestionably true that in the event of an accident the passengers would perish along with the driver. Arnold Toynbee has expressed the same idea more vividly: "No annihilation without representation." But whatever the formulation, it merely raises the problem without contributing to its solution. How is one to grant the passengers representation while negotiating a tricky stretch of road? As to the delay in using directional signals, the danger is real but inseparable from that of a misunderstanding or of the risk that an aggressor will not let himself be deterred. Once again we come back to the eternal question of who can deter whom, from what? in what circumstances? and how? Are the Europeans better able than the United States to deter the Russians from minor aggression? It is understandable enough for them to want to have their say and not to trust the driver blindly where their own lives are at stake. But unexceptional though these principles may be, the best way to put them into practice is far from clear.

General Gallois, of course, read the whole episode as a striking confirmation of his pet theories—the efficacy of small forces and the inability of a big power to protect a small one. Forty medium-range missiles installed in Cuba, and here the greatest country in the world is shaking in its boots. Who from now on could still venture to maintain that atomic forces, however limited in number, are worthless?

As usual, this reasoning contains one ounce of truth

and several ounces of casuistry. The forty missiles installed in Cuba were comparable to American missiles
installed 180 miles from Leningrad, or rather 180 miles
from launching pads for space ships and experimental
military rockets. To render the analogy even more precise we would have to assume missiles capable of by-
passing Soviet warning and detection systems. The extent to which Cuban-based missiles would have upset
the balance of forces has been discussed by the experts
at some length. Their primary effect would have been
to cancel the delay of at least fifteen minutes counted
on by those in charge of U. S. defense in the event Soviet missile launchings are detected by satellites, or
missiles in flight spotted by radar. As a first-strike
weapon, these forty missiles would have added substantially to Soviet capability for weakening the American retaliatory apparatus.

Their psychological impact would have been even
greater. The United States would have lost face if the
Soviet Union had proved itself able to defy it within
the immediate proximity of the American mainland.
But to compare, even by implication, the Soviet missiles
to the fifty Mirage IV bombers in the south of France
is to display a remarkable virtuosity in disregarding
essential differences and confusing the seizure of a forward position by a major power with the acquisition of
a few first-strike weapons by a minor one.

Besides, the Cuban experience teaches, if anything,
the difference between Soviet missiles in Cuba and
acquisition of an independent deterrent by the Cuban
Republic. Kennedy did not tolerate Soviet missiles in
Cuba, but he would have tolerated Cuban missiles even
less. If even a few missiles in the hands of a minor

power can frighten a major one, as has been stressed time and again, then it follows that no small country will be able to acquire such missiles unless it be under the protection of a big one. France is able to have an incipient deterrent thanks to the Atlantic Alliance. The major powers will stop the dissemination of nuclear weapons well before proportional deterrence in its extreme form has been put to the test.

On the other hand, the Cuban affair has in two different ways demonstrated the need for combining conventional and nuclear arms; local superiority in conventional arms allowed White House strategists to adopt the use of force in proportion to the objectives aimed at, starting at the bottom of the escalation scale, without firing a shot, by the simple proclamation of a "quarantine," while making it plain that they were ready to scale every rung of the ladder as high as was necessary. But let me repeat that the case was unique and far too well suited to American plans to be wholly convincing. [A Soviet attack with conventional arms in Europe would start at a much higher rung of the ladder and meet with far stronger resistance than that which Soviet cargo ships or even a few submarines could have put up against the U. S. Navy.] The fact that the Russians did not want to risk a nuclear war for the sake of maintaining their missile base in Cuba does not prove that the Americans in turn would recoil from such a risk if it were a matter of saving Europe from complete Soviet domination. To the extent to which the Cuban experience contains any lesson at all, it tends to confirm the American thesis: the protection afforded by a big power's deterrent is validated by balance or at least partial balance at lower levels.

The Cuban experience reveals still another function of conventional forces. Once the missiles were withdrawn, the Cuban Republic could defend itself in the same way that neutral countries always have in the past; in other words, it could exact from any potential aggressor a price disproportionate to the expected gain, even to the point of leaving nothing but ruins to be occupied. Obviously, the United States could wipe out the Cuban Socialist Republic and all its cities and inhabitants with a few thermonuclear bombs, but if Cuban leaders had the requisite courage,[13] they could refuse to surrender even without Soviet support. Confronted by a small nation without retaliatory capability and equipped only with conventional arms, a large one has no choice other than to attempt blackmail, morally and politically repugnant ("Surrender or I'll atomize you"), or to mount a conventional assault. I consider it rather likely that many a country, instead of seeking salvation in a costly and vulnerable small deterrent more apt to attract punishment than to inflict it, will come to rely on defensive weapons, i.e., weapons designed to bar physical occupation of its territory.[14]

The international situation, as outlined, does not warrant the heat of the arguments within the Atlantic Alliance. Proponents of divergent or conflicting theses carry on as if one kind of strategy would increase the likelihood of minor aggression while another was bound to bring about ultimate escalation. In fact, however, the Berlin crisis was the only one since President

[13] In all probability they do have it.
[14] In the long run such defensive weapons may include tactical atomic arms.

Kennedy's inauguration in 1961 that seriously endangered world peace. The strategy worked out to cope with the probable course of that crisis was graduated response. The West, rather than the Soviet Union, would have had to take the initiative in any recourse to force, which means that force would initially have remained limited.

Although each of the participants in the Atlantic debate tends vastly to exaggerate the implications of whatever strategy he happens to oppose, the disagreement itself is genuine; it involves a multiplicity of dimensions, it will be pursued inexorably, and there is as yet nothing to indicate that it will end in accord.

The argument stems from three sources: *geography, politics,* and *strategy.*

Between the Soviet and the Atlantic blocs there exists a physical asymmetry whose significance U. S. strategists tend to underestimate. The Soviet bloc constitutes a unified land mass; theoretically one might conceive of hostilities conducted along the outer frontiers of the empire not directly involving the Russian heartland, but even if the satellites did not have to depend on Big Brother for support, the Soviet Union and the sovietized countries of Eastern Europe would continue to be linked by a sense of solidarity[15] far more spontaneous than the affinities between the United States and Western Europe, where one partner is in direct contact with the potential enemy while the other is several thousand miles away.

Missiles, of course, can traverse these thousands of

[15] This, of course, applies only to the military and geographic aspects. Psychologically, the peoples of Eastern Europe do not seem to have been converted to Russian-imported communism.

miles within a mere half hour. But precisely for that reason they have only to be neutralized, and the United States becomes safe once again, restored to its preferential position of arsenal and last reserve. The strategy expressed by the McNamara doctrine aims at *minimizing the risk of the use of the only weapons to which the American mainland is really vulnerable.* And this strategy, regardless of whether or not it is the most effective one, appears much too closely identified with the strictly national interests of the United States not to arouse European suspicions. To keep hostilities from escalating means turning Europe into both the theater and victim of operations, with U. S. participation limited to an expeditionary force. Geostrategy, one might say, favors disagreement, whether groundless or well founded, between the partners on either shore of the Atlantic.

But even if the United States were to behave with the greatest of wisdom, and the driver of the automobile were to inspire total confidence, the passengers would still resent the place accorded to them in the Atlantic Alliance. Almost the entire American deterrent remains under completely American command. NATO is headed by an American general, appointed in fact by the President of the United States though chosen in theory by all the Allied governments.

The discrepancy between the resources devoted to national defense by the United States on the one hand[16] and by the Allies, either singly or collectively, on the other, is so vast that U. S. military and civilian

[16] The national defense budget of 50 billion dollars is twelve times the French budget, more than five times the total budget of all other NATO members combined.

chiefs inevitably exercise a preponderant influence in Atlantic councils, especially in matters concerning strategy. In the eyes of a traditional statesman like General de Gaulle, Atlantic interdependence (or Atlantic association) is sheer window dressing, barely veiled hypocrisy designed to camouflage Europe's reduction to political vassalage by the United States in the guise of protection. As long as the countries of Europe are content to let the United States retain a monopoly of the weapons regarded as decisive, they will be dependent protégés, if not satellites.

This quarrel was bound to erupt sooner or later, once Western Europe had rebuilt its ruins and regained its self-esteem. The passion with which it is being pursued, at least on the surface, stems from the McNamara doctrine (and the manner in which it was presented) as well as from the policies of General de Gaulle.

The McNamara doctrine, even when completely understood, stung the sensibilities not only of many a Frenchman and German but also of other Europeans quite ready to leave the responsibility for thermonuclear arms and their use to the United States. The Gaullists saw its prime purpose as an attempt to block the French program of atomic armament by denying the deterrent value of any small force to the point of denouncing such a force as an added hazard because its vulnerability would restrict it to a one-time sudden, massive countercity strike. Somehow the counterforce strategy seemed made to order, pulled out of a hat and timed so as to administer the *coup de grâce* to French ambitions. To Germans it constituted a demand for greater efforts in the field of conventional arms as a result of the "option" whose exercise the United States

intended to reserve for itself, or the "pause" which it
was eager to obtain following the onset of hostilities.
(In the meantime, what would become of the territory
on which hostilities had begun?) Finally it was inti-
mated, at least by the theoreticians if not by those actually in charge of strategy, that a kind of balance in
strength of the armies of the two blocs was the real objective and that this could actually be accomplished
much more easily than the experts advising the Eisenhower Administration had led us to believe. The 175
Soviet divisions, it seemed, exist only on paper or, more
precisely, on the books kept by the West; less than half
of them are full-strength divisions equipped with modern weapons. The number that could be committed in
Central Europe would be smaller still. The day NATO
was able to put thirty well-equipped divisions on war
footing in the field, even a full-scale offensive could be
repulsed without recourse to tactical atomic weapons.
Europeans immediately had nightmare visions of fighting for weeks in improved 1945-style combat, with
Washington—quite correctly, moreover—dubbing this a
"limited war." At the end of this particular path some
foresaw the complete withdrawal of all atomic weapons from Europe, and although responsible circles in
Washington denied any such intentions, several of the
theoreticians not working for the government but in-
fluential in the administration were openly recom-
mending the "disatomization" of Europe. This formula
would in fact afford the Big Two maximum latitude
right up to the last moment in deciding whether or not
to commit nuclear weapons and would thus spare them
the devastation bound to be inflicted upon both frag-
ments of Europe located between the Atlantic coast

and the Soviet border. Instead of putting the accent on the need to prevent escalation, the American spokesmen might have emphasized more than they did that graduated response strengthens rather than weakens deterrence. Sometimes it seems as though preventing minor hostilities from automatically escalating is the only thing that matters to them, while Europeans regard the second function of graduated response—that of enhancing the credibility of the retaliation or resistance threat by providing alternatives other than holocaust or passivity—as far more important. Europeans tend to dwell on deterrence because any war seems to them an unmitigated disaster; Americans think both of deterrence *and* use, because the failure of deterrence has for them entirely different consequences according to the strategy of use adopted.

The *principles* of the American strategic doctrine seem to me unassailable and, in due time, I think that they will be accepted by most countries, at least those able to translate them into practice. It is contrary both to common sense and to elementary prudence to stake everything on the threat of massive retaliation and to revive time and again the choice between passive inaction and total disaster. As nuclear powers multiply, the American doctrine of massive retaliation propounded in the early nineteen-fifties will lapse into oblivion; Europeans will begin to realize, if they have not already done so, that the strategy of graduated retaliation is both less immoral and more efficient than that of massive retaliation. But if in the long run the American system of thought seems to be the only feasible one, this does not mean that the conclusions that American theoreticians derived from it in 1962

or 1963 are necessarily self-evident. Even if we assume them to be theoretically correct, European reservations in turn are *easily justifiable by the geographical
situation of the European half of the Atlantic bloc* and
by the *dependence on the United States* to which the
non-dissemination of nuclear arms has reduced the
European continent.

Let us consider the conceptual system of the American strategists, designed to enhance the plausibility of
deterrence while at the same time minimizing the risk
of extreme escalation. Given Western parity or superiority at all levels, security would be as near perfect
as it ever can be[17] in an imperfect and dangerous
world. But if parity at the level of conventional weapons is unattainable, then it becomes pointless to refuse
to employ tactical atomic weapons either for deterrence or for attack.

First of all, such insistence would be theoretically
justifiable only if the strategy of use announced in
advance could actually be put into practice—if, in other
words, NATO troops could fight equally well with or
without tactical atomic weapons and if they were numerically strong enough to afford the military commander the choice of the fatal "option" for at least a
certain number of days. Anyone proclaiming a strategy that is manifestly beyond his capabilities courts
the risk of results drastically different from those intended. But the technological problems involved in
this twofold capability required of NATO troops are
difficult, to say the least, although a layman cannot
venture categorical opinions about what would happen

[17] The security of the West, that is; the Soviets might feel
differently.

if these divisions, after a few hours or days of combat, had to switch from deployment adapted to conventional arms to the organization necessitated by the use of atomic weapons.

Furthermore, the opinion presently prevailing among American analysts, according to which a distinction ought to be made between conventional and tactical atomic weapons, is based on two arguments, both valid but neither decisively convincing in the present situation of Western Europe. The sole distinction on which the U. S. and the U.S.S.R. can automatically agree without explicit communication is that between conventional and atomic weapons. Overpopulated Europe, on the other hand, is especially ill suited to the use of tactical atomic weapons. This argument obviously applies to the strategy of use; but the problem is to gauge what influence a prior notice of intent to maintain these distinctions will have on deterrence.

That the difference between conventional and atomic weapons is the most clear-cut one and that, at least in theory, it offers the best chance to avoid misunderstandings would seem to me beyond dispute. But the same strategists who believe in the possibility of maintaining distinctions between counterforce and counter-city strategy (and of discerning from the enemy's strikes the nature of his intent) ought not at the same time to accept escalation from tactical atomic to thermonuclear weapons as almost inevitable. There are, of course, circumstances in which one could imagine combat operations in Europe without recourse to tactical atomic weapons (for instance, if the West, as a result of Soviet encroachments upon Berlin, were constrained to use force). Likewise, in case of a Soviet raid aimed at creating a *fait accompli,* NATO troops must have the necessary strength to counter it effectively with only conventional arms. But aside from these two hypothetical situations (the second seems strangely improbable, the first was more likely in 1961–62 and may again become acute), it would be hard to see why the West should not attempt to deter a Soviet attack in Western Europe by threatening recourse to tactical atomic weapons. This threat does not add substantially to the risk of their actual use (the reduction of this risk is alleged to be of paramount concern) because use of these weapons is in any event highly probable; and it may help to prevent a possible misunderstanding on the part of the aggressor—who might misinterpret all the multitudinous and subtle precautions taken against an almost inevitable course of events as simple lack of fiber and determination.

Of course if we were to suppose that Western Europe and the United States had joined to form a single state, the unified government of this Atlantic world might conceivably hesitate to place tactical atomic weapons into its first line of defense; it would base its security on a combination of a major army deployed along the borders and reprisal weapons behind the lines or dispersed at sea. But even this unrealistic hypothesis of a single sovereign state governing the entire Atlantic world does not resolve the doubts. If the enemy were to use conventional forces as a "sword," what would the situation be if it came to a "pause," or to a resumption of bargaining? Would the aggressor keep the territory seized? The *fait accompli* is, after all, one method of aggression still feasible in the atomic age, and as long as tactical atomic weapons are needed to insure against this risk, it would seem dangerous to be overly specific about unwillingness to use them immediately, even if the Atlantic Alliance formed a single sovereign state.

This applies even more to the actual situation, with Western Europe divided into a number of sovereign states and the nation in charge of strategy, the United States, quite naturally concerned, above all, with averting escalation to a level where its own territory would become involved. In these circumstances, overemphasizing the difference between conventional and atomic explosives, stressing the reinforcement of conventional arms and refusing to install medium-range missiles on European soil to offset those deployed by the Soviets in large numbers along their western border might ultimately arouse a sense of danger in Western Europe and suggest to a potential aggressor that hostilities could remain confined to the area extending from the Soviet border to the Atlantic—i.e., between the privileged sanctuaries of the Soviet Union and the United States—much as in Korea the area between the Manchurian and Japanese sanctuaries was staked off and devastated in three years of war during which the North Koreans, supported by the Chinese, and the South Koreans, supported by the Americans, fought each other to a draw.

In other words, agreement on a joint strategy between Europeans and Americans presupposes two conditions that have not yet been met: Europeans must accept the American conceptual scheme and relinquish the illusory doctrine of massive retaliation. Americans in turn must not concentrate their attention exclusively on the strategy of use and on ways to avert escalation, but must make an effort to view the situation from the European perspective and eventually make concessions to their allies' frame of mind.[18]

Even if agreement could be reached on a common strategy, the old problem would remain a stumbling block: whose finger is on the trigger? The Americans regard it as essential for the Atlantic deterrent to be unified, that is, subject to a unified single command at the moment of crisis. The strategy of graduated use controlled at all times by clear-sighted resolve, as conceived by the Americans, precludes the existence of more than one center of decision and cannot accommodate national forces which, because of their vulnerability, can strike only once and as complete units or not at all. Since General de Gaulle's conception, on the other hand, implies above all else the independence of the deterrent as well as of the political and strategic uses to which it is put, no reconciliation in depth is possible between Washington and Paris at this time.

The Nassau agreement, it seems to me, added new aspects to the controversy. The Kennedy Administration kept explaining in private that if the benefits of the McMahon Act authorizing communication of classified information to certain countries[19] were extended to France, it would be more difficult in the future to reject similar demands from Germany. This argument has never seemed very persuasive to me, since, by fearing to discriminate against Germany in favor of France, the Americans actually continued to discrimi-

---

[18] Once again, these speculations have up to now yielded no results.

[19] Countries that have already made sufficient progress by themselves.

nate against France in favor of Great Britain.[20] Moreover, the Federal Republic, under the Treaty of Paris,
agreed not to manufacture atomic arms and it would
need many years to catch up if it were to start now. It
has no territory suitable for testing and could not defy
the veto of both Russia and the United States unless it
had surrendered to a quasi-Hitlerian madness.[21]

After the public announcement that the Skybolt project had been abandoned,[22] Kennedy could not in good
conscience refuse Macmillan a substitute, i.e., the Polaris missiles. In return, he obtained British agreement
that the British deterrent force (a so-called multinational force) would be placed under NATO command in time of peace, as well as a promise of support
for the multilateral force; this latter promise has so far
remained conditional. From Washington's point of view
the accord had the merit of curtailing the independence, theoretical rather than factual, of the British
deterrent, and of offering France a status equal to that
of Great Britain. It could have been interpreted as putting an end to discrimination against France in favor of
Britain; but General de Gaulle chose to read a different
meaning into it. He saw it as further justification for
his decision to oppose Britain's entry into the Common
Market. Britain had revealed herself to be Atlantic
rather than European; the Macmillan government, suddenly deprived of the one weapon upon which it had

[20] President Kennedy in August 1963 justified this discrimination on the basis of French rejection of a joint strategy and of
even a multinational force.
[21] Such an attempt would, in fact, be more insane than anything Hitler ever tried.
[22] The Americans claim that the British Defense Ministry had
been notified several months earlier.

counted to maintain an independent deterrent, turned to the United States rather than to continental Europe to obtain a substitute, at no matter what cost.

The multilateral force, once the French had rejected it and the British were reconsidering their promise to participate, was offered only to countries that did not want it in place of what they did want.

This multilateral force—Polaris missiles on surface vessels with mixed crews—whose military efficiency is debatable to say the least, has at best only countercity capability. It thus merely adds strength in an area in which the United States already has more than enough power, without meeting either the strategic or the political objections raised in Europe. In point of strategy, most Europeans believe that intermediate-range missiles installed in Europe would constitute a more effective reply to Soviet missiles in regard to both deterrence and use. The Americans, however, turned this down because they wanted, it seems, to retain complete control of retaliatory capabilities. They insist on keeping these missiles outside Europe proper, on vessels integrated into the total American network as part of a deterrent whose use would be subject to veto by the President of the United States.[23]

Of course this multilateral force is unquestionably of some value when it comes to refuting those who believe that the atom has rendered all alliances obsolete. To a certain extent it may help to strengthen American commitment in Europe and disabuse the Russians

[23] Two technical arguments are also advanced: the cost of protecting missiles installed in Europe, and Europe's population density, which makes it impossible to limit losses and spare cities once the missiles are used or become targets of enemy strikes.

of any notion that the United States would recoil from extreme risks unless it were itself directly and immediately involved. What reasonable Europeans fear, however, is not so much that the United States will abandon Europe, but that its strategy, by stressing increased flexibility of response, would in the end unduly enlarge the zone of operations below the atomic threshold. And since, according to American war plans, the multilateral force can intervene only in countercity action, i.e., in the final phase, it is not likely to be of much help in allaying the fears—whether unfounded, sincere, or otherwise—aroused in certain Europeans by the trends of American strategy.

True, it could be argued that this multilateral force has the merit of introducing Germans and Italians to the rudiments of atomic technology and strategy, thus forestalling the demand for participation that the Federal Republic is bound to make sooner or later. But it remains to be seen whether offering the Germans a 40 per cent financial participation today in a multilateral force that conforms neither to their strategic concepts nor to their political goals will really block their demands or whether, on the contrary, it will give rise to claims that already stir anxiety because it is known that they would have to be rejected.

Let me conclude that as of July 1963, when the three principal members of the atomic club—the United States, the Soviet Union, and Great Britain—signed the agreement to suspend nuclear tests in the atmosphere, in space, and under water, Britain had not surrendered the independence of her deterrent, France was as determined as ever to acquire one of her own, and the

American strategy was accepted by all members of the Alliance because they had no other choice, but with no unanimity prevailing either among the experts or among the statesmen.

This analysis raises two questions: one is whether and in what manner true agreement can be restored among the members of the Atlantic Alliance, and the other is whether and to what extent the Alliance will remain viable failing such agreement.

The agreement must cover two points—the strategic concept and the finger on the trigger. As concerns the first, I shall limit myself to general remarks, lacking as I do the special competence required to go beyond them. The problem, posed in abstract terms as I have repeatedly done here, does not seem insurmountable. NATO cannot do without a certain number of divisions capable of conveying the initial message of force that the West may be constrained to deliver, and capable also of repelling raids or probes that the Soviets might risk if present circumstances were to change. How many divisions do these functions require? I can imagine the generals arguing the point, but I find it hard to believe that the figure thirty, which is still ritualistically invoked in speeches by American political figures (Dean Acheson, for instance), has any magic significance or that it is based on any rigorously scientific proof. In the abstract, thirty is of course preferable to twenty-five; but whether the marginal yield of those five additional divisions is significant in terms of foreseeable contingencies can be effectively proved or disproved only by those having access to the work done by the General Staff sections.[24] On the other hand, there should be no disagreement that these divisions need to be effectively equipped and deployed so as not to leave major gaps or weak spots.

These arguments, as we have seen, focus mainly on the potential recourse to tactical atomic weapons; they are exacerbated by the intentions ascribed to American strategists rather than by the measures the Americans have actually taken, if it is true that stockpiles of atomic warheads in Europe were increased by 50 per cent over the past two years. A difference of opinion on this issue undoubtedly exists between Europeans and Americans, rooted in their respective geographic situations and also, to a certain extent, in the divergence of national interest between continentals on the one hand and non-Europeans (the United States and Britain) on the other. Any compromise solution is open to criticism, and it would probably be necessary to go into details and know the secret plans in order to decide which compromise seems least objectionable and most likely to maintain a threat of escalation without at the same time rendering it inevitable. But however equivocal and debatable any such compromise may be, I do not think that it need be quite so irksome once Europeans learn to trust the principles of the American doctrine and the Americans in turn make an effort to understand the mentality of the Europeans, for whom no war will ever be quite as "limited" as it may seem on the other side of the Atlantic.

[24] General Valluy, former Commander in Chief of Allied Forces, Central Europe—i.e., in a good position to formulate an opinion—believes that the figure of thirty divisions is based on solid arguments.

Far more serious, on the other hand, is the argument over the unity of command. Broadly speaking, a solution may be sought in three different ways: first, reforms in the structure and command of NATO designed to give Europeans a deeper knowledge of the American apparatus and a sense of participation in the preparation and conduct of strategy; second, formation of a European force closely tied in with the American force; and finally, American surrender of the monopoly of command, and unification of the deterrent through the co-ordination of the American force with the French and British national forces.[25]

The most elaborate solution of the first point is that proposed by Alastair Buchan. It is based, to put it briefly, on the difference between the French and English meanings of the word *control*.

Control, in current English usage, means possession, command, mastery. Like the word *power,* it is one of those vague terms that the English and Americans seem unable to do without and that add to the ambiguities. Just as *power* may, according to the context, cover both the means and the exercise of power, its actual possession as well as its instruments, so *control* covers the whole range from possession through command to inspection.

Arms control suggests to the Russian negotiators checking on, or inspecting, disarmament agreements, whereas in a very broad sense the term covers mastery over available arms, reduced in number if possible,

[25] In order to complete the list we would have to repeat here the various versions of the NATO multilateral or multinational force.

increased if necessary for the sake of peace and stability.

Contrôle in the French sense involves neither possession nor command but the right to be let in on the conception, formulation, and elaboration of strategy, which by this very fact will become a joint one (doctrine of use, responses planned in various circumstances, relations between various types of weapons).

More specifically, the Europeans could make an immediate contribution to a nuclear force under NATO command, an atomic force whose function would be to prevent major military moves in Eastern Europe. The British V-bombers could carry out such a function far more efficiently than they could their present assignment of long-distance reprisals far inside Russian territory. Likewise the Mirage IV bombers, whose range of action is insufficient for any genuine strategic reprisal missions, could someday be integrated within this force which, while remaining under NATO command, would be guided in its commitment by plans worked out, if not by Europeans alone, then at least in agreement with them, since in theory they should meet the specific needs of Europe.

But although such a preventive nuclear force is a major component of Mr. Buchan's theory,[26] it far from exhausts it. The focal idea is to give Europeans, at least in an initial phase, a sense of participation in the Atlantic strategy and of control (in the French sense of the word). The reforms he proposes include reorgani-

[26] He proposes the organization of a special general staff at the same level as SACEUR, to be called SACAIR, whose task it would be to plan for and assume command of all nuclear weapons assigned to these preventive functions and based either on European soil or in adjacent waters.

zation of the NATO Secretariat, to transform it into an effective center for discussion and planning among the Allies. The post of Supreme Military Commander, which now involves both the function of military adviser to the NATO Council and that of operational commander in chief, would be divided. An American NATO Chief of Staff, either directly subordinate to the Secretary General or his equal in rank, would be appointed and he would be given three assistants, one French, one German and one British. The *standing group* would be replaced by a NATO representative to the Pentagon. The operational commander, who would take orders from the NATO General Staff, could be European.

In addition, this NATO reform would be complemented by a wholly European organization within the framework of Western European Union, whose purpose would be to study weapons standardization and evaluate the apportionment of military levies among the various countries. Finally, the Europeans would participate in the Pentagon's strategy planning and would eventually be admitted to that most sanctified of inner sancta, the Omaha Headquarters of the Strategic Air Command.

The fundamental assumption underlying this solution is that if the Europeans acquired control, in the French sense, of joint strategy, they would stop asking for control in the English sense. In other words, once they felt that they had made a genuine contribution to the strategic concepts and operational plans, they would be willing to leave operational responsibility to the American leaders. This fundamental assumption in turn supposes that U. S. strategists would take into account the objections raised by Europeans against some aspects of their present doctrine.

If the French Government came to accept this solution, the United States and Britain would probably go along with it.[27] But as long as General de Gaulle remains President of the Republic, the plan will run headlong into a French veto, and without French participation it can hardly be put into practice. An organization of this kind, whether conceived as a step toward Atlantic supranationality or simply as a closer co-ordination of national policies and strategies, is not acceptable to the French Government. And whether or not the government has actual veto power, French opposition or simply non-participation would be enough to reduce the value of the reforms to near zero.

A second solution often proposed is that of a wholly European deterrent within the framework of Western European Union. Henry Kissinger has recently come out in support of this idea, and Professor Strausz-Hupé, James E. Dougherty and William R. Kintner have presented it in a book entitled *Building the Atlantic World*.[28] It is possible that General de Gaulle might have supported Britain's entry into the Common Market if one of the conditions had been British-French co-operation in the atomic field with an American blessing. Since the 1963 crisis, the idea has become largely academic, but as it is not inconceivable that circumstances may someday render it relevant again,

[27] How far would they go? A moot question.
[28] There are different versions of this plan, according to whether the European deterrent is to be strategic or tactical, consisting of medium-range missiles or mainly of weapons for battlefield use. See James E. Dougherty, *European Deterrence and Atlantic Unity*, ORBIS, Vol. VI, No. 3, 1962.

there may be some point in outlining briefly both its advantages and dangers or difficulties.

A European deterrent financed jointly by the Six plus Great Britain would attain the threshold of effective deterrence and therefore would obviously be better than independent French or British forces during the coming decade. For instance, Alastair Buchan, although personally opposed to this formula, admits that the Seven by means of their own industrial and financial resources could within a few years acquire a diversified deterrent consisting of 500 strategic delivery vehicles, i.e., bombers and intermediate-range missiles, either land-based or installed in surface vessels or submarines. The seven countries combined, he points out, spent 13,462 million dollars for defense in 1962, or about one fourth of the U. S. budget. An additional 3 or 4 billion dollars amounting to a budget increase of between 25 and 30 per cent would enable them to acquire a substantial retaliatory force. This increase would raise the national defense expenditures from 5.5 to 7 per cent of the national income, which is still far below that of the United States (about 11.25 per cent) and the Soviet Union (18 per cent).[29]

The greatest technical difficulty is to find testing grounds, now that the European empires in Africa no longer exist. Europe has no areas comparable to sparsely populated Nevada or Montana, where the Titan and Minuteman bases are located, and must look to the far Pacific for a suitable spot. But the technical

[29] These figures seem questionable to me. The Soviet percentage is an approximation. The French and British figures are already above 5 per cent. A 20 per cent increase would raise political problems.

obstacles are minor compared to the explosive political problems created by friction between the European countries themselves, between Europe and the United States, and between Europe and the Soviet Union.

The question of control of the trigger arises in connection with the European deterrent just as it does with the Atlantic one. Even if the European force were to be essentially a tactical one, would the French lightly grant the Germans the right to decide when to use it? If the force is to be strategic, the ambiguity of "control" in the French sense (theoretically divisible) and of control in the English sense arises once again, the latter being as hard to divide among Europeans as between Europeans and Americans. Perhaps the difficulties would be less in that the European countries constitute a physical unit while Europeans and Americans are separated by thousands of miles of ocean, but they would be increased by the quasi-equality of European states, which precludes the sort of arbiter that has always, throughout history, been essential to the proper functioning of a federation, and at the same time makes it difficult to agree on whose finger would be on the trigger.

Furthermore, Germany and Britain, if they do participate in a European deterrent, will do so only by agreement with the Americans, who for the time being are opposed to the idea. McGeorge Bundy has declared that American opposition to ineffectual and non-integrated national deterrents might not automatically extend to a genuinely unified and multilateral one, effectively integrated with the American force that would of necessity be predominant in the total nuclear defense of the Alliance. The reference to integration does not encourage the assumption that Washington would accept the real independence of even a unified European deterrent. If such a force were to be organized, not against explicit American opposition (this is inconceivable, for the time being) but in the face of American reservations, it might well result in a loosening of ties between the two parts of the Alliance, and at least implicit notice to the Russians that a European initiative would no longer commit the United States in any and all circumstances.

Alastair Buchan suggests that the Soviet Union would take preventive measures against the organization of such a force, because they would fear it would provide the nucleus of a German deterrent or at least be subject to undue German influence. But personally I believe that a Soviet reaction need not be feared except in the event of open U. S. opposition to a European force. Its organization, as I said, would require the consent, however reluctant, of the United States; otherwise neither Britain nor the Federal Republic would take part in the experiment. The formula of a European deterrent, though temporarily sidetracked by the course of events, does not seem to me definitely dead and buried. The deterrent would not necessarily be strategic or subject in all its elements to a unified command. After all, NATO accepts a multinational force, and Europe could, in an initial phase, put national forces under a unified command exactly as is done in the Atlantic Alliance. A fact acknowledged even by opponents of a wholly independent European deterrent is that the European countries share common problems of defense differing in certain respects from those of the United States. No one up to now has come up with the perfect solution that meets at the same time the specifically European needs and the higher necessity of a close link to the United States, but the best chance to find one is to forget neither aspect of a problem staggeringly complex, at least in theory.

The third solution—the simplest if not the best—is the one now adopted for want of anything better. First Britain, then France, have followed the United States and the Soviet Union and have acquired, or are about to acquire, a small-scale national deterrent. From the viewpoint of the Atlantic Alliance this is obviously the worst possible solution, since France is now spending billions to produce weapons and discover secrets that the United States already possesses. The same amounts spent on conventional arms would contribute much more to collective security, at least during the period in which the French force would not deter the Soviet Union from moves that the American power failed to block. But as long as the goal of French policy is the (at least theoretical) ability to make sovereign decisions concerning war and peace, as long as non-integration and massive retaliation remain the accepted French doctrine, none of the technically possible solutions has the slightest chance of practical success.

The demand for military independence, regarded as an end in itself, essential to the state and to its grandeur, can be satisfied only by a wholly and exclusively national deterrent.

This is undoubtedly General de Gaulle's objective. It also explains why no reconciliation will be possible as long as American strategists cling to unity of operational command as the guiding principle of any Atlantic strategy while General de Gaulle regards the non-integration of the French national deterrent as the very essence of his entire policy. Of course he may some day agree to a measure of co-ordination sufficiently close to integration to satisfy the Washington strategists. The English deterrent retains its nominal independence by being subject to national command in the event of a crisis (though it is under NATO command in time of peace), but it is dependent on the American detection and early warning system. In fact, although Washington may conceivably have come to regret the previous administration's decision to share atomic secrets with Britain, American strategists do not consider that the British force is a serious violation of the principle of unified operational command. If France should ever envisage the use of her independent deterrent in a spirit similar to that of Britain, or if she succeeds at least in convincing American leaders that her deterrent is not meant to serve the purposes of a diplomacy conducted without regard to the Atlantic Alliance and that it can take its place in a jointly planned strategy, there might be some chance of reaching an agreement that would take both positions into account. The dominant factor of the coming decade is that the security of the whole of Europe will continue to depend on the American deterrent and on the presence on European soil of some divisions from overseas. Less important, but irreversible, is the fact that France will not officially surrender her independent deterrent.

Is it true, then, that the manifest disagreements within the Atlantic Alliance prove that all alliances are doomed, because even the greatest nuclear power can

no longer protect an ally? Not at all. France, though
dissenting within the framework of the Atlantic Alliance, nonetheless remains under its protection. No
European country has any doubt that its security will
depend on the American deterrent for at least another
fifteen years. Some may believe this security to be
more precarious now than during the earlier phase of
American invulnerability, but few would regard a small
independent force such as the French or British deterrent as a significant addition.

Is it probable that military establishments will become smaller as the means of destruction grow ever
more disproportionately large? This paradox is not altogether inconceivable but will not come about until
the smallest country has an invulnerable capability to
destroy the largest one—until, that is, Monaco acquires
the secret of lethal retaliation against the Soviet Union
or the United States. Mankind is still some distance
removed from the so-called Unit Veto System. In terms
of policies, for the next twenty years all countries will
be either on the sidelines of the nuclear conflict between the Big Two or else protected by one or the
other.

It is true, however, that alliances between countries
that cherish their sovereignty are put to a grueling test
by thermonuclear weapons. But the non-credibility of
the threat brandished by a major power for the benefit
of its protégés is at present more of a rationalization
than an expression of profound intent. Any country is
bound to be uneasy about leaving exclusive responsibility for decisions affecting its life and death up to
another, even if it be an ally. If this ally will not share
the fate of his protégés, they will profess fear of possi-

ble rash action on the part of their protector; but if the latter becomes equally vulnerable, they will express the opposite fear. The protector, in turn, will attempt to formulate a strategy minimizing the risk of suicidal involvement, that is, in the present context, of a thermonuclear war. But this again leads the protégés to fear other types of conflict. The major nuclear power will finally seek an implicit agreement with its enemy partner, equally interested in avoiding a nuclear holocaust. The allies of either rival are unlikely to be victimized *militarily* by such an implicit or explicit agreement, because it can be reached only on the basis of the status quo and mutual respect of vital interests, but they may become its *political* victims.

The truth, far more complex, is that at this time nations can neither rely wholly on alliances nor entirely do without them. This is why present diplomacy resembles that of the past more than some observers are inclined to believe. The novel aspect is the danger of dissolution to which the alliance is exposed as the junior partners rebel against the senior's exclusive command and attempt to regain some mastery over their destiny.

This, however, does not justify concluding that the Atlantic Alliance is doomed. It does mean that the links between its members are bound to weaken if, in the absence of an agreement on joint strategy, several countries decide to play a fully independent nuclear game. To this extent the national deterrents risk precipitating the very danger that theoretically they are supposed to prevent or compensate for, i.e., the decline of the American deterrent.

Finally, the political future of the Atlantic Alliance and of the world as a whole will not be decided merely by the existence of weapons that are not used, no matter how powerful their impact upon an international system determined not to use them but unable to do without them.

6

Logic and Paradoxes of the Strategic Theory

From the preceding analyses, some involving inter-governmental conflicts and all more or less linked to changing circumstances, I can now pass to a theoretical synthesis comprising the novel elements of contemporary diplomacy and strategy as they are affected by nuclear arms.

The idea of the classical philosophers that "sovereigns in relation to each other are in a state of nature" is still as true as ever. The proposition should be acceptable even to positivists; for the state of nature is the opposite of civil society, defined by the existence of laws, courts of law, and instruments of government legally empowered and practically endowed with the means of unconditional coercion. It would even be permissible to apply the concept of *social system* to the agglomeration of "political units" (referred to as "states" in our day) that are in more or less regular contact with one another, provided we bear in mind that a diplomatic system displays one feature that distinguishes it from all other social systems: the legitimacy of the resort to force by each of the component units, or the absence of a power entitled in principle and able in fact to enforce a verdict and thus to prevent the members of the system from taking justice into their own hands.

All international systems known throughout history have striven in one way or another to blunt the implications of this anarchy; the measures have ranged from discipline imposed by big powers on small ones to commitments, attempts at maintaining a balance of sorts, and pacts such as the League of Nations covenant or the United Nations charter, whose explicit purpose is to banish war as an instrument of policy. But the essential anarchy of the system has never been overcome—neither in fact, because no supragovernmental authority ever has had the means of enforcing decisions against a state, nor in law, because all legal texts have contained reservations and loopholes safeguarding the time-honored privilege of individual states to take justice into their own hands, or subtly restoring this privilege in spite of international organizations designed to curtail it.[1]

Nothing has changed in this respect. Moreover to judge from our brief experience thus far, thermonuclear arms have made it even more difficult to substitute a legal or political order for the chaos of power struggles. It has always been difficult to imagine the application of collective security, meaning collective action by the international community (or a sufficiently large part thereof) for the purpose of imposing certain restraints upon a major power;[2] but what was once difficult has

[1] See *Paix et Guerre Entre les Nations,* p. 544 ff. and p. 704 ff.
[2] The reason is simple: a state can be constrained only by the threat of force. The states not directly involved are reluctant to go to war for the sake of law; but unless the international community is determined to employ force, a big power would see no reason to yield.

become practically impossible now that big powers
have thermonuclear warheads and the means to deliver them over thousands of miles within a fraction of
an hour. Furthermore, it now seems that the ability of
major powers to keep small ones in check is paralyzed
by the incommensurate violence of the weapons available; witness Albania, which is to the East what Cuba
is to the West. Unquestionably the dichotomy of thermonuclear power is one of the factors accounting for
the impunity with which dwarfs are allowed to flout
giants. Even though Russia and the United States are
fundamentally agreed on not wanting China to acquire
the atom bomb, they seem unable to stop the Chinese
nuclear program,[3] and it is far from certain that even
by concerted action as allies the Big Two could successfully exploit the atomic threat in order jointly to
rule a submissive and frightened mankind.

The role of the United Nations is real but does not
extend to effective intervention in the duel between
thermonuclear powers. Instead, the international organization is being used by them for a variety of
purposes, such as sanctioning agreements already concluded, publicizing reciprocal recriminations, proclaiming the pristine innocence of their intentions before
the world or avoiding direct intervention in areas or
conflicts of marginal importance. Peace, at the higher
level of big-power relations, is being maintained not
by law but by force.

But if political relations between states remain a

[3] Journalists already talk of a Russian-American alliance for
the purpose of *physically* preventing China from completing her
program. There can be no question of it at this time. See Nor-
man Jacobs, "Freezing the Balance of Terror," *The New
Leader,* Aug. 5, 1963.

function of power politics, the weapons of massive destruction have nonetheless modified the conditions under which force may be used or, to put it more accurately, *the conditions under which the use of force may be threatened and actually carried out*. Thermonuclear arms together with ballistic missiles introduce three elements that are qualitatively new to human history as a whole. The first is the *magnitude of the destructive power of thermonuclear arms*. This qualitative mutation is illustrated in the Russian reply to the Chinese Communist charges: *The explosive power of a single thermonuclear bomb is greater than the total explosive power of all ammunition used in all the wars of the past, including the first two World Wars of this century.*

The second new element is the *permanence and almost instantaneous nature* of the danger. As I have pointed out, surprise attacks are no novelty; archaic societies as well as the relatively stable international systems of higher civilizations have all made new rules of procedure designed to stress the distinctions between peace and war, create a climate of confidence in time of peace, and prevent sneak attacks. Though violations of these rules have often resulted in temporary gains, sudden aggression has rarely proved decisive in the long run, since there has always been time subsequently to mobilize forces for a counterattack. In theory, a massive attack by missiles with thermonuclear warheads would probably not prevent a first-rate power[4] from visiting terrible retaliation upon an aggressor; but this retaliation would be merely post-

[4] For the time being, however, this does not apply to second-rate powers.

humous, so to speak. Moreover, if the first strike destroyed the better part of the victim's retaliatory capability, there might be some question about the rationality of a response that, though inflicting punishment for a crime, would also provoke the aggressor into finishing the job of annihilation.

With this we come to the third new element of the thermonuclear age. Absolute victory as defined by Clausewitz in his day meant disarming the enemy, beyond which point the victor was able freely to decide on the fate of the vanquished and kill him if he so desired. But from now on the entire population of a belligerent country might well be exterminated before the end of hostilities. No weapon, conventional or atomic, in the present stage of technology, can protect a nation from death. *It is no longer necessary to disarm a country in order to annihilate it.* Of course the aggressor must disarm his enemy, in the sense of destroying his reprisal weapons, if he wants to escape retaliation. Nevertheless these weapons no longer serve the traditional functions of protection that fortifications, guns and soldiers served in the past. Preventing the physical occupation of one's country is no longer sufficient to guarantee the safety of civilians; but the air raids of the Second World War, carried out with conventional explosives, terrible though they were, did not endanger the physical survival of the nation as a whole. Today there is no longer any limit to the damage that major powers can inflict upon one another and upon all mankind without having to move a single soldier or pay the slightest attention to the millions of men in uniform who, armed with conventional weapons, continue to guard the borders of the 110 so-called states that constitute the United Nations.

These three radically new elements are instrumental in determining the three major concepts of the strategic theory, concepts that in turn suggest the three responses so far worked out to the triple challenge of *monster weapons, permanent alert* and *annihilation of entire nations without the need first to disarm them.* The first is *deterrence,* symbolic of the effort to substitute the threat of force for its actual application; the second is *stability,* replacing the obsolete notion of balance of power and designating the theoretical situation in which no nation would be tempted to make use of its weapons; the third is *arms control,* including both the arms policy in advance of a crisis and the conduct of diplomacy and strategy during the crisis itself. In pre-atomic days it was rationally conceivable to aim at absolute victory in terms of disarming the enemy and thereafter to limit the fruits of the victory. From now on, a reasoned conduct of war stopping short of extreme violence has become essential wherever the confrontation involves countries in possession of these frightful means of destruction. This, moreover, applies even to countries unafraid of enemy reprisals, if their aim is to rule or to exploit rather than merely to destroy. Thermonuclear arms cannot be used to clear the way for occupation, and nobody, not even a student of Tacitus, would dare proclaim that he was bringing peace if what he brought was the atomic desert.

The concept of deterrence is central to strategic theory because present-day diplomacy wants to substitute, once and for all, the threat of force for the use of it. But, precisely because this threat is not supposed to culminate in its actual execution, the strategy involves an intrinsic contradiction: how can one persuade the adversary that the threat will be carried out if the potential victim is perfectly well aware of the consequences not only to himself but also to the other party? The problem, as we have seen, may be subdivided into the questions of who can deter whom, from what, in what circumstances, and by what sort of threat.

To none of these questions can there possibly be a simple answer, even if the problem is posed in terms of schematic models involving a strategist whom we shall refer to as "rational." And the uncertainties proliferate once this theoretical strategist is replaced by a collection of real leaders with their differing value systems, political doctrines and world perspectives—to say nothing of the problems of deducing from Khrushchev's current pronouncements the actions of Mao's successors.

Let us return to the model presented by G. H. Snyder in his book *Deterrence and Defense*,[5] which postulates only two contending states. One of the opponents wants to upset the status quo by grabbing from his rival some asset such as a province or natural resource. His decision would be based on four factors: (1) the value of his objective; (2) the cost to him, given various possible responses by the other side; (3) the probability of these various responses, and (4) the probability of winning the objectives according to each possible response.

The defense, in turn, would examine four factors in

[5] Princeton, 1961.

the event of an aggression: (1) the value of the objective the aggressor wants to attain; (2) the cost of fighting; (3) if fight is decided on, the probability of successfully holding on to whatever is at stake, and (4) the consequences of this decision on the future course of rivalry with the aggressor and on the probability of future enemy attacks.

Finally, the potential aggressor must attempt to gauge what is likely to be going on in the mind of his chosen victim at the moment when the latter is actually confronted with the onset of operations. The four questions asked by the victim of the potential aggression suggest various measures by which the defender may invest with credibility an action that by itself and ahead of time would seem too irrational to be plausible.

The first step consists of persuading the adversary that there is no cheap way for him to attain his coveted objective because its possessor attaches to it an immense value. All through the years of the Berlin crisis American statesmen made countless commitments in both word and deed, the sole purpose of which was to impress upon Soviet leaders not only American resolve but also the impossible situation in which American leaders would find themselves if they were to yield. Beyond a certain point the ostensible stakes are, in fact, transformed by the answer to the fourth question, the psychological consequences of a local defeat. Who would ever again take American guarantees seriously if after all its many promises the United States were to sacrifice not merely two million Berliners but its own honor? Who would ever again trust its promises?

Let us assume hypothetically that the defender

makes two modifications in his own thinking, and that
these changes will influence the decision of the potential aggressor if he becomes aware of them: the defender commits his honor and future along with the
original stakes, thus vastly increasing their value, or
else he invests materially insubstantial stakes with spir-
itual values that by their very nature are not susceptible to measurement, thus amplifying the fatal consequences that retreat or defeat would entail for him.
The aggressor may not, of course, always let himself be
convinced in just any circumstances; doubts persist in
the wake of even the most unequivocal declarations,
because a paradox intrinsic to deterrence requires the
defender to brandish the most extravagant threats, although he may not necessarily proceed as he had
vowed to do if they fail to deter the enemy after all.
In other words, the potential aggressor must constantly
take into account the probability of various types of
response on the part of his victim in the face of aggression as well as the cost and probable development of
the crisis in various hypothetical situations (Questions
2 and 3).

The cost to the aggressor will obviously be far
greater if the response is total and the victim resorts at
once to massive thermonuclear retaliation. But as the
growing invulnerability of reprisal weapons tends to
reduce the advantages of a first strike, this type of response becomes less and less plausible even where a
thermonuclear power is attacked. The enormity of
devastation that even a medium-sized force is capable
of inflicting suggests an abstract proposition that
agrees with probability theory: if the stakes are huge,
it is better not to play even if the probability of having

a bad hand is no higher than 1 in 100 or even 1 in 1000. But players are not always deterred by the cost of a bad hand that seems so remote. Total response may theoretically prove more costly to the aggressor (as well as to the defender) than anything short of it; but unless the defender can invest the threat of total response with sufficient probability, he will actually improve the efficacy of deterrence by forcing the aggressor to contemplate the probability of a more moderate response, with the cost and the uncertainties implicit in this sort of operation.

Now we must look back at the defender's Questions 2 and 3: confronted by the *fait accompli* of an aggression he had tried to deter, what conventional means can he muster to repulse it locally? What forces would the aggressor in turn have to mobilize in order to crush the resistance of troops armed with conventional weapons? Ample means available for the defense of the objective at stake and a high probability of resistance make the outcome of limited operations correspondingly more doubtful, so that ultimately the aggressor will face a choice between an immediate massive attack, with its likely consequences of retaliation, and renunciation of his plans.

The terms *offensive-defensive* and *deterrence-defense* are used in several different senses and may lead to ambiguities; definitions are therefore necessary. What I outlined here was a duel between two adversaries, one of them eager to upset the status quo and thus taking a diplomatic offensive, the other wanting to deter the first from action. This was the case when the Soviet Union wanted to change the Berlin situation, and the West, under the leadership of the United

States, was on the defensive. In military terms, deterrence refers to efforts by one side to prevent a given
move by its adversary. In this sense, strategic deterrence is part of a defensive diplomacy. But defense in
the traditional sense of the term—i.e., the use of force
to deny an aggressor access to a given territory—far
from conflicting with the diplomacy of deterrence is,
in fact, an aspect of it. Territorial defense is the opposite of reprisals, and in the thermonuclear age territorial defense is conceivable in two forms—with either
conventional or tactical atomic weapons.

Let us first take a small country on the fringes of the
rival power blocs and lacking any and all reprisal weapons: will such a country be forced to capitulate if
threatened by a thermonuclear power? Given the new
factors of mass destruction, the theoreticians' answer
was affirmative at first, and in the abstract this remains
true. But having admitted that there can be no such
thing as perfect security in this world, one must concede the partial efficacy of territorial defense. The
thermonuclear power could in fact destroy the small
country; but to what purpose? If the people and their
leaders show the requisite courage, their defensive capability will force the aggressor armed with his superbombs to choose between costly conquest and futile
destruction. A weak retaliatory capability might in
some cases prove more of a danger than a protection.
World opinion now supports American efforts to keep
nuclear arms out of Castro's hands; but assuming—
however improbable it seems—that the United States
were to threaten extermination of the Cuban people if
Castro refused to capitulate, the indignation of man-

kind, as well as the American conscience, would prevent execution of the threat.

Switzerland and Sweden, it seems, planned and perhaps still are planning to acquire atomic weapons, but, at least where Switzerland is concerned,[6] they seem intended for defense rather than retaliation. Small-caliber atomic weapons could lend support to territorial defense by making invasion even more costly and thus render the ratio between cost and return even more unfavorable. By betting on defense rather than on retaliation, it might not be altogether impossible to reconstitute in the thermonuclear age a situation comparable to traditional neutrality, but with a difference —the risk that the big power will not be deterred by the attempted intimidation and, if the small power refuses to yield, will at least partially carry out the threat of annihilation.

It might be objected that possession even of small-caliber atomic weapons almost inevitably implies a certain retaliatory capability; after all cargo planes, too, can be used to deliver rather substantial bombs. But by not acquiring missiles, long-range bombers or large-caliber bombs, a state serves notice that its nuclear arsenal is intended for defense rather than retaliation.

The place of defense within a strategy of deterrence is at the core of the current controversies in the Atlantic Alliance. Without wishing to repeat the arguments examined in previous chapters, I want merely to formulate the fundamental proposition in the most abstract terms possible. Whether we are dealing with an isolated country or with an alliance, the means of terri-

[6] The Swiss in a referendum defeated a proposal to prohibit their acquisition of atomic weapons.

torial defense are an element essential to the strategy
of deterrence, and their scope cannot be determined
in a general and abstract fashion. The true choice is
not between deterrence and defense but between defense and retaliation. If a medium-sized country wants
to acquire a retaliatory capability vis-à-vis a major
power, and if it is determined to have an independent
policy and remain aloof from all alliances, the strength
of its defenses must increase in proportion to the proximity of the potential enemy and the latter's ability to
inflict damage far beyond that which threatens him.

If neutrality is the aim, a country favored by geographic factors may limit itself to a defensive capability based on the absurdity of an aggression that would
destroy the object at stake without resulting in gains
for the aggressor. But a small power seeking to assure
neutrality by means of retaliatory capability against a
big power would incur a twofold risk: *either* a categorical demand by the big power to dismantle this
capability *or* the eventual choice between suicide and
surrender, because the small power would lack means
to respond to intimidation or warnings in any way
other than by unleashing suicidal action. For a nation
wishing to participate in world politics, retaliatory capability is even less of a substitute for defensive capability. In theory, every country and every coalition
ought to possess the means of defense adequate to
counter any type of aggression short of the threshold beyond which thermonuclear retaliation becomes
plausible.

But whatever the role of territorial defense in the
world of today and in the thermonuclear world of tomorrow, deterrence nonetheless remains the major

strategic concept, a fact that modifies the classical theory of Clausewitz in one essential point. Clausewitz compared diplomacy to a business transaction on credit, in which war is the ultimate cash settlement; all outstanding obligations must be honored on the battlefield and all debts paid. *The thermonuclear age does not do away with this distinction between prior commitments and the moment of truth; but now the moment of truth is the crisis rather than war,* because contemporary theoreticians can no longer accept the battlefield settlements once regarded as inevitable. Their aim, on the contrary, is to prevent engagements from ever taking place.

Stability, the second key concept of the present theory, can be defined as follows: *A situation will be considered militarily stable if neither of the countries confronting one another is tempted—or would be tempted if it were acting rationally—to resort to force even if it is not content with the existing state of affairs.* The concept of stability can be derived from the concept of deterrence in that, according to the preceding definition, it designates *a situation of reciprocal and general deterrence.*[7] It may also be defined in contrast to the *political instability* of the world as of now or to the traditional *balance of power* idea. It constitutes the response to the challenge of permanent danger; ballistic missiles need only half an hour from the heart of Asia to the coast of the United States, but the strategists ought to be able to devise a system of warning and of retaliation that in turn can become operative at a moment's notice, so that peace will be maintained simply

[7] Meaning of the level of both large and small wars, and of conventional as well as atomic weapons.

because a first strike, with either conventional or nuclear arms, will clearly be against the best interests of
both sides.

Let us start with a retrospective glance at the relationship between political and military stability as it
existed in the past. An international situation was considered stable if the various countries accepted it. In
the abstract, two variables regulated this stability—the
intensity of feeling about unsatisfied claims, and the
ratio of strength between satisfied and dissatisfied
countries. The greater the would-be aggressors' sense
of superiority in both actual and potential strength,
the greater the threat to peace. On the other hand, the
vanquished were less clamorously recalcitrant and
their recovery was less likely to jeopardize the new
order if they did not feel that they had been treated
unjustly in the wake of their defeat. After 1918, the
victors were able neither to satisfy the losers nor to
keep up the margin of superiority essential to the
preservation of peace.

Even in the thermonuclear age, stability, defined in
strictly military terms, still depends partly on the political variable—i.e., the degree of dissatisfaction displayed by the defeated ex-enemies. But after 1945 the
cost of a possible war led theorists to minimize or almost ignore the political variable in their quest for
military stability, a situation where both sides would
abstain from the use of force whatever the intensity of
the grievances.

Politically, the international system since 1945 has
been afflicted with fundamental instability of a radically different sort from the kind that characterized
the European system between 1918 and 1939. The

losers of the last war, Germany and Japan, have been rendered powerless. The conflict among the victors has given rise to what we call the cold war with its three facets—*ideological rivalry, de facto territorial boundaries in Europe tolerated but not officially recognized,* and *competition for the allegiance of the non-aligned countries.* International relations since 1945 have unquestionably changed far more rapidly and radically than they did between 1918 and 1939; the dissolution of European empires, the victory of communism in China, the emergence of some sixty genuine or fictitious states, are all historical events that make the squabbles over Alsace-Lorraine or Ethiopia seem downright fatuous. But although this is an era of revolution, with the international system rent by ideological passions and the pace of industrialization ever more rapid, the relationship between the major powers, always decisive in its influence on the alternatives of war and peace, has for the past eighteen years been such as to make all-out war wholly irrational.[8] For both Russia and the United States—neither of them lacking in land or resources—such a war would have involved an incommensurate risk for the sake of a potential gain, even apparent world domination. Therefore it is hardly surprising, from the point of view of traditional theory, that the conflicts between the Big Two or the two power blocs have not transcended the limits of the so-called cold war.

The contrast is striking: on one side of the coin, the absurd European boundaries, dividing Germany and Berlin, and revolutionary turmoil in many of the under-

---

[8] This would have been true even without nuclear weapons.

developed countries, and on the other, the West's firm
intent to prevent recourse to force wherever possible
and to prevent the use of nuclear arms in any event.
The present international situation certainly does not
inspire hope of a peace based on the satisfaction of
everyone's aspirations; but the weapons' destructive
power is such that the dream of an unprecedented
peace based simply on the fear of war tempts everyone
sooner or later. Clear analysis unfortunately tends to
show that complete military stability—i.e., the certainty
of avoiding violence, founded on nothing but reciprocal deterrence—is beyond the realm of possibility.

At moments of crisis in pre-atomic days, chiefs of
state would compare their own resources to what they
thought the enemy could mobilize. The balance of
power was central to diplomatic theory for the simple
reason that it described the conditions necessary for
the system to function; no state or group of states could
be allowed to acquire a superiority so crushing as to
make it predominant and thus put an end to *autonomy
of action*, the supreme goal of each unit within the
system.

The balance of power, prerequisite to the proper
functioning of diplomatic systems, failed in the long
run to assure either the security of the several states or
their collective peace. The balance was never lastingly
maintained, and even where it seemed to be, it merely
served to encourage the machinations of discontented
parties. The more evenly balanced the opposing forces
of states or coalitions appeared to be, the more easily
an ambitious leader or an expansionist nation could
come to cherish notions or delusions of superiority. It
has actually never been possible to measure military

strength with anything like rigorous accuracy, not even in modern times when it is vaguely proportionate to production, especially to industrial production. Not only did leadership and luck influence the outcome of battles, but the quality of the contending armies remained by definition unknown until tested in the field. Furthermore, each system included a number of uncommitted states whose eventual choice in favor of one side or the other usually helped to tip the scales.

If all countries had pursued peace and security as their primary aim—which has never happened at any time in history, public statements notwithstanding—they should have welcomed the undisputed superiority of one particular state, ruling absolutely enough to discourage stray impulses toward revenge and at the same time moderately enough not to become unbearable. Basically this was Bismarck's design. But it, too, turned out to be an illusion. The dominant state is bound to become unbearable because in the long run arrogance always wins out over moderation, in word if not in deed, and domination itself usually provokes a realignment of forces with consequent restoration of balance. At the beginning of that fatal summer of 1914 both sides believed in victory and, moreover, both turned out to be right after a fashion; the Germans won the war that everyone had been expecting, but not decisively; and the Allies in turn won the other war, unforeseen and triggered by the inordinate duration of the original one, leading eventually to American intervention. In other words, a simple dilemma blocked the way to lasting peace in systems founded on power politics: either the balance seemed perfect, in which case each belligerent hoped for possible victory, or else

one side seemed manifestly superior and thus constituted a threat to the other. Security based on strength
is a mirage; if one side feels safe from attack, the other
will feel at the mercy of its enemy.

How much of this still applies in the thermonuclear
age? In abstract terms, two new facts are immediately
apparent. One is that uncertainty may no longer hold
the same psychological attraction as it did in the past.
When no one was able to gauge the precise ratio of
strength ahead of time, an adventure seemed tempting
by virtue of its very unpredictability; now that this
unpredictability involves fatalities on the order of tens
of millions, even the most adventuresome of leaders
might conceivably be inclined to caution. The other is
that stability through reciprocal deterrence no longer
requires equality, not even in theory; it is in no way
necessary to destroy the same cities twice or kill the
same people three times over. This is the line of reasoning that misleads excessively tidy minds into imagining
a kind of world-wide stability in which a multiplicity
of states will deter one another, with all differences
between dwarfs and giants leveled and everyone equal
before the absolute weapon. *For the time being* speculations of this type belong to the realm of science fiction. It is true that nuclear equality is not essential to
the balance of deterrence; but the weaker party must
still have reprisal weapons sufficiently numerous and
invulnerable to be able to inflict second-strike damage
considered unacceptable by the stronger adversary.
No one, of course, can accurately predict just what the
stronger will regard as unacceptable, and the less valu-
able the object at stake, the more deterring the effect
of even a limited threat. But it is doubtful, for instance,

whether Great Britain, the first of the small nuclear powers, has the minimum strength required to counter a threat by a big power and to restore the balance in the face of manifest inequality.

Even where the Big Two are concerned, reciprocal deterrence has never been perfectly stabilized. The element of uncertainty, which in the past attached to the efficacy of armies in combat, is now of a technical order. The immense thermonuclear systems have never had to operate under actual wartime conditions. The missile silos have never been battered by thermonuclear explosions. What would really happen in the event of a massive attack? Would the command and communications networks remain intact? Would the leader of a half-destroyed country insist on revenge rather than try to save part of his nation?

These technical and psychological imponderables relate to the least likely hypothesis of an all-out duel unto death; but even if we disregard them, the theory of stability still contains contradictions that, while different, are just as irreducible as those of the old balance of power. The contradiction at the core of the McNamara doctrine and central to controversies in the United States is merely a new version of the old contradiction between *domination*—considered unbearable by the lesser states—and *equality*, which is liable to give rise to an unacceptable spirit of initiative. In contemporary terms the contradiction involves superiority based on the exclusive or at least greater counterforce capability of one side, and *equality* based on the reciprocal invulnerability of both retaliatory systems.

This contradiction may, of course, be purely theoretical. Today, the Americans believe their weapons

have a certain strategic counterforce capability; but
the Russians, whether or not they agree with this estimate, do not feel seriously threatened. For one thing,
they are not worried about the Americans' starting a
war by a presumptive strike, and for another they are
convinced that they would in any circumstances salvage a retaliatory capability adequate to deter a direct
attack even by an enemy not inhibited by moral scruples and a democratic constitution. If we assume the
United States to be superior both in its ability to destroy enemy weapons in a first strike and in its ability
to destroy enemy cities in first and second strikes, stability at a higher level—i.e., the level involving actual
use of thermonuclear arms—is perhaps as great today
as the nature of the strategic duel will permit.

But it is equality, the second assumption, that leads
us straight back to the traditional instability; for the
growing invulnerability of retaliatory weapons tends
to make their use increasingly implausible. *Stability at
every level is impossible by definition.* If each side
keeps a few hundred missiles with thermonuclear warheads in practically invulnerable reserve, aware that
the other is doing likewise, then their actual use would
be tantamount to suicide for both.[9] Each has what the
theory refers to as a minimum of deterrence, in other
words, the ability to deter the other from launching
missile-borne thermonuclear warheads—but from what
else? The state of balance between the adversaries by
definition shrinks the zone covered by thermonuclear

---

[9] Destruction of some twenty major cities in Russia and the
United States would not mean the end of the world or even the
end of these two countries, but it would set them back years or
decades.

threats; as a result, a complementary deterrent is needed to check limited operations and surprise moves that cannot be prevented by a threat utterly out of proportion to the scope of the action.

Now if this complementary deterrent consists of conventional arms, the traditional uncertainties involved in the ratio of strength, quality of troops and ability of generals seem likely again to come into their own. But an added and far more serious element of uncertainty is inextricably related to the variety of levels at which one country may respond to the challenges of another. In the event of an all-out attack the uncertainty is mainly, if not exclusively, technical in nature; but what will be the response to a limited attack against one sector of a coalition? The qualitative diversity of weapons available, and hence the wide range of conceivable types of war, again precludes perfect stability; the idea of escalation complements the concept of stability.

The greater the stability at the level of ultimate weapons, the more uncertain it becomes at the level of conventional ones. The more the gap between limited wars and conventional arms on the one hand and nuclear arms on the other is stressed in both word and deed, the less reason there is to fear escalation. The less reason to fear escalation, the greater the probability of limited conflicts. Hence the tension among allies, some of whom are mainly afraid of all-out war while others worry just as much about limited ones. Hence, also, vacillations among pacifists, who wonder whether they now ought to be in favor of conventional wars as a way to prevent nuclear ones, or assume that peace is based on bilateral possession of invulnerable reprisal

weapons, or work for total disarmament to build peace
on foundations other than fear.

The United States, as we have seen, has in fact dis-
carded both extremist solutions. To threaten all-out
terror on any and every occasion is a risky procedure;
sooner or later a potential victim will refuse to submit
and thus force a choice between meek capitulation and
apocalyptic execution. But a solemn promise to the
effect that under no circumstances will the party concerned be first to use nuclear arms leads right back to
the uncertainties of power relations and wars between
states. The intermediate solution—relatively stable deterrence at a higher level, possession of a substantial
defensive capability without claiming an unascertain-
able equality, and maintenance of the threat of escalation by refusal to disavow progression from one type of
weapon to another—seems to me reasonable although it
is not beyond debate and does not eliminate all danger. Strategy, past and present, must choose between
dangers: reducing the risk of escalation increases the
temptation to use conventional weapons as a "sword"
under the cover of a thermonuclear "shield" (or under
the protection of reciprocally paralyzed thermonuclear
systems). If no distinctions are made between initial
operations and ultimate weapons, there is a risk of
ultimate escalation by accident or misunderstanding.
In short, *escalation is at once a danger that needs to
be met and a threat that could not and should not be
surrendered.*

This threat can be brandished even by a nation with
a weakened counterforce capability once the doctrine
of massive retaliation has been abandoned for good.
The strategy of graduated response, of which the coun-

terforce action is merely one element, aims at averting precisely this dilemma of unavoidable versus impossible escalation. It is, in fact, a way of warning the
enemy that his every bid, no matter how high, will be
topped.

The strategy of graduated response constitutes a
reasonable answer—though not necessarily always the
best one—to the contradiction inherent in stability, a
compromise never fully satisfactory to everyone. Designed to minimize the most monstrous of dangers
without substantially increasing risks comparable to
those of the past, it expresses the contradiction contained in the concept of escalation, a process simultaneously feared and exploited as a threat. It is this
very contradiction that defines the essential nature of
the thermonuclear duel: the opponents strive to obtain
certain results by making threats they do not intend to
carry out and, unable to agree to drop their threats,
try to go on playing the game while minimizing the
risks it involves to themselves.

The contradiction inherent in stability has led us to
the strategy of graduated response which, however, is
as much a part of *arms control* as it is of the *theory of
stability*. Arms control, in the widest sense of the term,
refers to the total effort aimed at preventing recourse
to force and, failing this, at limiting the scope of the
resulting violence. The strategy of graduated response
may therefore be regarded as *arms control during a
crisis*.

In an early phase American strategy was dominated
by the all-or-nothing, "go or not go" alternative. Luckily, the conditions that would have triggered mass
murder never came about; and the idea of war as a

thermonuclear spasm in which each side hits the other with everything at hand, causing fatalities by the tens of millions within a few hours, no longer haunts the mind even though Soviet doctrine has never officially given it up. If strategy is part of diplomacy in time of peace, why should it suddenly give place to a truly demoniac and demented frenzy at H-hour of D-day?

By virtue of its American origins and its inner logic, the strategy of graduated response is part of arms control. The concept of control, because of the ambiguities inherent in the English sense of the term, has sometimes been interpreted as an aspect or enlargement of the old concept of disarmament. Actually it would seem justifiable to stress *arms control* as the major concept, with arms reduction ahead of time and graduated response during the actual crisis as the two complementary components. The aim ahead of time is to achieve the greatest possible stability at all levels; during the crisis the goal is to avoid escalation to extremes which, given the weapons available, would involve monstrous destruction. But in both phases connivance or at least communication between the enemies is imperative.

There is no point in listing here the various measures, outlined vaguely or in detail by American specialists, that would enable the enemies to play the game of reciprocal deterrence strategy without *either* side's being handicapped and without their *both* risking mutual destruction. For the purpose of explaining the conceptual structure of the strategic theory, a few observations will suffice.

The direct cable link between the Kremlin and the White House now referred to as the "hot line" was, so far as I know, first proposed in the *Bulletin of the*

Atomic Scientists. This line has in the eyes of the world come to symbolize a secret understanding between the two heads of state, although actually it thus far represents merely the acknowledgment of an agreement limited to the prevention of a war in which the Big Two would be the first victims. In a crisis, who would most stand to gain from teletype negotiations? Up to what point is this direct communication compatible with the threat of escalation? There is no sure answer to these questions. As of now, the hot line is a safety device against accidents; in the near future it may become a safety device against bomb-toting troublemakers. But it also signifies a degree of agreement, not drastically new in itself but greatly accentuated by the horror of nuclear arms, that links the enemy partners—*at least providing that each renounces any hope of annihilating its rival.*

Furthermore, these enemy partners have a common interest in preventing the dissemination of atomic weapons. They are also eager not to hide from each other any facts bearing on their respective retaliatory capabilities so long as these tend to reinforce the deterrent value of whatever declarations or commitments have been made.

From this point of view, unilateral measures designed to curtail armaments may also contribute more to the security of both rivals than would a stepped-up arms race that could not affect the ratio of retaliatory capability and would merely aggravate mutual suspicion.

The paradoxes and logic of this strange world in which we live are summed up but not resolved in the connivance of the Big Two, political enemies who

nonetheless agree in wanting to avoid a struggle unto
death. The power of thermonuclear arms is incom-
mensurately destructive to the objective sought; the
threat is permanent and instantaneous; the object at
stake in any conflict would be destroyed if the belligerents carried their hostilities to extremes. Therefore the Big Two cannot afford to give in to their hatred and neglect their common interest any more than
they can afford to ignore their enmity, inevitable as
long as they preach mutually exclusive gospels and as
long as a third nation does not arise to challenge them
both and force them to make common cause.

The American theoreticians taught President Kennedy to see the world in terms of these concepts. The
American President, in turn, tried to convey this vision
to Khrushchev. The hot line and the partial test ban
were the first results of this effort.

Contrary to the hopes of those in quest of absolutes,
the strategic theory culminates neither in a simple lesson nor in a miraculous solution. The risk of violence is
inseparable from the multiplicity of sovereign states,
and also, perhaps, from man's social condition. Any theory of action, even if it involves extreme danger for its
practitioner, may under given circumstances yield certain advantages. To deter, in the ordinary sense, means
to scare; and anyone in possession of a small atomic
force who gives the impression that he is irresponsible
and unaware of what is at stake may for some length
of time exert an influence quite out of proportion to
the means at his disposal.

Just as Clausewitz, after postulating the concept of
absolute war, proceeded to introduce various factors

that widened the gap between absolute and actual war, so the contemporary strategist must take into account certain considerations that tend to make the world of thermonuclear duopoly less terrifying in fact than it would seem from the researches of the analysts.

All theories, even the most abstract, now suggest that the enormity of the risk imposes caution, where in the past the indeterminate nature of the power ratio was apt to lure bold men to adventure. So far it seems that the two major powers have adopted the simplest rule possible in order to avoid all-out war: to renounce recourse to arms—or at least to organized forces—to change the status quo. The Soviets in particular still talk and act as though the danger point were not so much progression from conventional to nuclear arms as a direct clash between Russians and Americans in any form. The world situation since 1958—with the exception of the Cuban episode—has evolved as though Khrushchev, after having vainly tried to obtain some concessions by brandishing his long-range missiles, had reached conclusions opposite to American theories and abstract logic and decided that the monster weapons made even local wars inordinately dangerous because it was impossible to predict where they would lead.

Even if Mr. Khrushchev has really drawn this conclusion from the thermonuclear stalemate, it would unfortunately be premature to conclude that either his successors or other nations possessing atomic weapons in the future will follow suit. It is important to bear in mind the circumstances in which the rivalry of the Big Two has taken place so far.

Any military operation in Europe, minor or major, involves immense risks because nothing less than the entire free half of the continent is at stake. Moscow's strategy in Europe is offensive, aimed at the disruption of the Atlantic Alliance, the withdrawal of American troops, and the reunification of Germany on Soviet terms and under Soviet auspices. But these objectives cannot be obtained by force. Tempting as it must have seemed to procure a first-rate triumph and chase Western troops out of Berlin by nothing more than threat of force, Khrushchev and the men around him have never gone beyond harassment and have refrained from taking a chance on translating the theory of the "thermonuclear shield" and the "conventional sword" into actual practice.

It is difficult to determine what has prompted this caution, whether it was the official Soviet doctrine of inexorable escalation, American superiority in thermonuclear power, or the pointed Soviet resistance to understanding the strategic subtleties in which American experts indulge with such apparent delight that it sometimes seems that they deliberately want to compound confusion and bait their enemies. Let me merely say that circumstances were auspicious for peace. The side on the offensive diplomatically and eager to advance (in this instance the Soviet Union) has, until now, been the weaker of the two in the thermonuclear duel; and though it has held conventional superiority at most points, it also has regarded war as indivisible and, for all its boasts, has not been certain of the invulnerability of its strategic force. Finally, neither opponent has been anxious to modify the status quo or else has not attached to any particular objective a value high enough to justify any great risk.

In spite of this stability favored by the comparative strength of strategic capabilities and the paradoxical asymmetry of respective doctrines, one crisis did bring the Big Two into a direct confrontation.[10] This crisis —disregarding unknown pressures to which Khrushchev may have been subject—can be explained (like the Korean War) only by an error of judgment in the realm of human psychology. There was no remote resemblance between the reality and the Kremlin's idea of what Americans in general and President Kennedy in particular were like. The strategy of deterrence is essentially a test of will power, an exchange of alternate threats and messages, or rather of threats bearing messages and messages pregnant with threats. Pure theory is schematic and involves ideal strategists, whereas a real-life crisis confronts two human beings. The strategic decision vis-à-vis a given country must take into account the probable reactions of that country as reflected in the thinking of those who rule it. Any instantaneous decision will also allow for the adversary's probable reaction as shaped by the type of personality that on the basis of past experience one is inclined to ascribe to him.

But substituting a flesh-and-blood strategist for the abstract mind that merely calculates the respective capabilities for destroying cities or reprisal weapons and incorporates the enemy's rational moves in its own calculations introduces additional grounds for both hope and fear. There is a chance of inaction where pure theory would counsel action, and a risk of misunderstanding in spite of all available means of commu-

---

[10] The Korean crisis took place before the era of thermonuclear duopoly, and both North Koreans and Chinese were interposed between Russia and the United States.

nication. It is possible that Khrushchev sent his missiles to Cuba because he was mistaken about his opponent's character (psychological misunderstanding). Perhaps he withdrew them immediately because he regarded escalation as inevitable. Perhaps President Kennedy refrained from demanding withdrawal of all Russian troops from Cuba because he wanted to help his adversary save face so as not to goad him into a precipitous act of folly that he feared Khrushchev might have preferred to backing down (however incompatible this may be with the Communist principle of not letting oneself be provoked). Finally, by his very moderation President Kennedy may well have conveyed a message drastically different from the one he intended and merely confirmed Khrushchev's already low opinion of American leaders and their political acumen.

In short, an exchange of messages is no guarantee of understanding. Misunderstandings are not necessarily lessened by continuous communication. Besides, perfect mutual understanding would make the game impossible to play; and the game remains essential as long as thermonuclear states are engaged in power politics. Why is perfect understanding neither possible nor, perhaps, even desirable? Because beyond a certain point the use of thermonuclear arms can never seem wholly rational if both sides are vulnerable, even if not equally so. It is almost impossible to imagine what a war fought with all available weapons would be like without coming to the conclusion that only a madman could possibly unleash it. Therefore it has sometimes been considered preferable to act the madman in order to be taken seriously rather than pretend wisdom in a madman's game—a depressing thought, even if it does contain a grain of truth, and deadly in its implications for mankind as a whole. The Big Two have succeeded in minimizing the dangers of the thermonuclear age precisely because they have never abused this logic of insanity.[11]

Will the two sides go on observing simple rules and utmost caution? Will the defenders in the game of diplomacy keep stressing the distinction in degrees of violence which the aggressors tend to question? Will future members of the atomic club resist the temptation of "rational irrationality"? It would be futile to hazard guesses; all we can do is take stock of the multiple and contradictory effects resulting from the thermonuclear factor.

The threat of war, even of thermonuclear war, is part of current international relations, but war itself would in most instances be contrary to all rationality and, far from being an extension of politics, would put an end to it altogether. This contradiction accounts for the connivance of enemies as well as for the suspicions among allies; for the impossibility of reconciling the enemies and of continued trust among allies; for

[11] The well-known statement by Christian Herter before the U. S. Senate is a striking example of a moderate formulation giving rise to misunderstandings among allies as well as, perhaps, among enemies. He said that he could not conceive of a U. S. President involving the country in all-out nuclear war unless the U. S. itself were in danger of being completely devastated, or at least unless the enemy had actually taken certain actions pointing toward such destruction. Interpreted literally this statement, coinciding in time with increasing American awareness of U. S. vulnerability, did not mean that Europe would be abandoned in the event of aggression but may merely have suggested graduated response. It did more to upset the Europeans than to reassure the Russians, however.

disarmament talks as well as the arms race; and for the obsessional fear of war coupled with the hope born of anxiety that this war for which both sides are arming will never have to be fought.

At the same time the irrationality of total war and revolutionary dynamism are contributory factors in the proliferation of all forms of violence; in abolishing traditional forms of peace as well as conventional war; in rendering the old balance-of-power concept ambiguous by the very polymorphism of wars, and in reducing the monster weapons to impotence while limiting the autonomy of states that regard themselves as sovereign.

Two events may best symbolize the shadow that thermonuclear weapons cast upon the world of diplomacy—Cuba's impunity, and the Moscow-Peking rift. Never before have the giant powers had so much trouble constraining their small and weak neighbors, but never before have the countries in possession of the decisive weapon been so determined not to share their secrets, even with their closest allies.

The rift between Peking and Moscow was not caused exclusively by the problem of nuclear arms; but we know for a fact that in 1957 their friendship and alliance were intact and that at the international conference of Communist Parties the Chinese delegation moved to have the pre-eminent leadership of the Russian Party officially recognized in the charter of the world Communist movement. That same year a Chinese-Russian agreement was signed stipulating delivery to China of an atom-bomb model. The following year Khrushchev angered Chinese leaders by suggesting a summit conference in connection with the Middle East crisis. Chinese operations against Quemoy and Matsu in August 1958 ended in a resounding failure. Khrushchev quite obviously was not anxious to let the recklessness of Mao Tse-tung and his entourage drag him into an adventure against a "paper tiger with atomic teeth." In 1959 the Soviet Union unilaterally abrogated the atomic treaty of 1957. In 1960 Russian technicians left China. In the meantime, the "great leap forward" as well as the commune experiment had ended in failure, and the Chinese Party was driven into an increasingly militant stance that Moscow stigmatized as dogmatic. In August 1963 Russia, the United States and Britain signed the partial test ban, which China correctly interpreted as being directed against her.

No one can precisely determine the degree to which nuclear arms have been determining factors in this conflict, but the disagreement originated in the more flexible diplomacy adopted by Khrushchev and in the Chinese moves Moscow regarded as dangerous. Whenever the diplomacy of an ally risks triggering a nuclear conflict, the principal partner in the alliance will reassert his monopoly on nuclear arms or, failing this, will invoke discipline in matters of strategy. In return, Khrushchev was forced to grant the countries of Eastern Europe increasing autonomy in such areas as agricultural collectivization, industrialization, and even trade relations with the West. China would in all likelihood have obtained similar concessions—aid and internal autonomy—if only she had been ready to submit to the strategic discipline that Russia, as the possessor of thermonuclear weapons, insists on enforcing. China, however, was too ambitious to trade away for good the age-old privilege of sovereign states—i.e., the right and power to choose war or peace—and too ambitious to forgo weapons of any kind, even those destined only to prevent their own use.

It is possible that a movement dominated by political ideology could under no circumstances have adjusted to two religious capitals, despite the seemingly unlimited flexibility of that ideology. But although it occurred within the context of a clash susceptible to ideological formulations, the break dealt with the very essence of international relations, the matters of strategy and weapons.

7

Final Considerations

Europeans are fond of complaining that American strategy changes at least as often as the President. John Foster Dulles, or perhaps President Eisenhower, introduced the ideas of "massive retaliation," of the accrued yield per unit of expenditure ("more bang for a buck") and of retaliation in case of aggression—the location and the means to be determined by the United States rather than by the aggressor. The use of tactical atomic weapons for the defense of Europe was approved in 1953; but in 1961 Europeans were asked to concentrate their efforts in the area of conventional arms. Some diplomats or statesmen too busy to follow American research and theoretical developments are wondering whether tomorrow will bring another shift in attitude and how much confidence can be placed in any doctrine, be it massive retaliation or graduated response, liable to be swept away by the next wave of intellectual fashion or by the next man to win the elections.

I have tried in this book to relate the various strategies to diplomatic situations, to differentiate between theoretical analyses and the doctrines that derive from them, to outline the established results—a way of thinking, a concept of diplomacy in the thermonuclear age —and to avoid confusing these working concepts with notions prevalent at present but nonetheless debatable, such as the risk of escalation attaching to the use of tactical atomic weapons, or the danger of a major war in Europe, considered possible by some experts.

Besides, strategy and tactics have always depended on the means available. The novelty resides not in the evolution of strategic doctrines that has accompanied changes in weapons and delivery systems, but in the speed of technological development. The dictum that "only fools never change their minds" has never been more to the point than when applied to strategists who blindly cling to their pet notions, regardless of technological revolutions and changes in the power structure.

In this final chapter I shall try to look ahead, and for this purpose I shall examine in sequence the four variables governing the future of the game of deterrence: *the number of countries possessing atomic or thermonuclear weapons,* or the problem of proliferation, *the qualitative arms race,* or development of new or improved arms and means of delivery, *the possible political developments,* involving either a realignment of nations or else the aggravation or relaxation of present conflicts, and finally the *consistency or inconsistency* of strategic doctrines. This book focuses mainly on the fourth variable, but we shall be able to view it in its proper perspective only after briefly examining the other three.

According to American theorists, one interest that has for the past few years been common to both Russia and the United States is the non-dissemination of atomic arms or, to put it another way, the perpetuation of the thermonuclear duopoly (or quasi-duopoly). The Kennedy Administration from the start sought to prove this to Khrushchev and his men, but in the first phase they met with only limited success.

The following facts may shed light on the reasons for Soviet reluctance. In an early phase in 1961 Soviet technicians considered it clearly vital to continue testing in order to "catch up" (as American technicians put it), to perfect their knowledge and their bombs—in particular, to produce bombs of very large caliber and to test the effects of very high altitude explosions. They prepared their test series behind the screen of a moratorium unilaterally proclaimed by each of the Big Two in succession. After the Russians and Americans had both run a series of tests, negotiations still remained deadlocked over the issue of underground explosions which from a distance might be mistaken for seismic tremors, thus requiring on-the-spot inspection. In 1962 Khrushchev proposed three such inspections annually; subsequently he withdrew this offer, finally agreeing to sign a treaty that would ban testing in the atmosphere, in space, and under water while authorizing underground tests, i.e., tests verifiable only by inspection in Soviet territory. I should add that the treaty itself contains a clause that restricts its effectiveness—each signatory may abrogate it on three months' notice if unusual circumstances (of which the signatory is sole judge) make a resumption of testing essential to the national interest.

The very least that can be said is that Soviet leaders do not seem to have given very high priority to the test ban; they may worry less about the spread of nuclear weapons or they may not believe that it can be effectively prevented by agreements of this kind—or possibly both. At any rate, rather than consent to on-the-spot inspection, they preferred to exempt underground tests, the most useful ones for their present purpose, that is, the development of small-caliber weapons. And they signed the ban, aimed chiefly at China, only after disputes aired in public had made the rift within the Communist camp an established fact. It may have been Khrushchev's quarrel with Peking that ultimately persuaded him to sign this agreement that commits him to nothing. As long as he had cause to hope for a reconciliation or compromise with Mao Tse-tung, he refrained from adding fuel to the fire; but once Mao started aspiring to the leadership of the Communist International and posing as the defender of Marxist-Leninist orthodoxy against Moscow revisionism, there was no longer any point in trying to spare his feelings. On the contrary, the test ban, while it may not keep the Chinese from acquiring the atom bomb, did provide an ideological weapon against them in the eyes of the non-aligned countries who, perhaps spontaneously, perhaps because of the impact of Soviet propaganda, are unanimously opposed both to nuclear tests and to nuclear arms. China's refusal to sign the treaty, no matter how legitimate in terms of national self-interest, relegates her to a position of moral inferiority in the contest between the two centers of Marxism-Leninism for the ideological allegiance of the Communist Parties in the non-aligned countries.

The efforts of President Kennedy do seem eventually to have made some impression on Khrushchev.

Following the Cuban crisis, the Russians agreed to installation of the "hot line," symbolizing the kind of communication between enemies essential to the prevention of ultimate disaster. Even prior to the Cuban crisis a preliminary limited agreement for three years, 1963–65, was reached at Geneva in June 1962 between Hugh Dryden, Deputy Director of the National Aeronautics and Space Administration, and Anatoli Blagonravov. It provided for co-operation between Russia and the United States in weather and communications satellites and in the study of the earth's magnetic field.[1] Moreover in Moscow on May 22, 1963, Glen Seaborg, chairman of the U. S. Atomic Energy Commission, and Andronik Petrosyants, his Russian counterpart, signed a three-year agreement on co-operation in peaceful uses of atomic energy, exchange of scientists, and some joint research.

The co-operation between the leading nations of the two blocs has timidly opened a small breach in the wall of hostility and mistrust. Will it prevent the spread of atomic arms, as the Americans, if not the Russians, seem to hope? Two studies have been devoted to this problem: one is *The Nth Country Problem and Arms Control* by W. Davidon, M. Kalkstein and C. Hohenemser;[2] the other, published under the auspices of the Institute of Strategic Studies, is entitled *The Spread of Nuclear Weapons*, by Leonard Beaton and John Maddox.[3]

The first ends on a pessimistic note, at least if increased membership in the atomic club is regarded as

[1] Final negotiations took another year; the agreement was signed in Geneva in August 1963.
[2] Washington, D.C., Jan. 1960.
[3] London, 1962.

deplorable. It sets up three categories; the most advanced consists of countries that have reactors as well
as the scientific and economic resources necessary for
the manufacture of atomic bombs. Twelve countries
are included: Belgium, Canada, China, Czechoslo-
vakia, France, the German Federal Republic, East
Germany, India, Italy, Japan, Switzerland and Sweden. The second category—countries that have the
economic resources and the technological know-how
but are somewhat deficient in scientific personnel—includes eight countries: Australia, Austria, Denmark,
Finland, Hungary, Holland, Poland, and Yugoslavia.
A final category consists of countries that have adequate economic resources but are short on scientific
and industrial capacity—Argentina, Brazil, Mexico,
Norway, Spain and South Africa.

This study, although it aroused a sector of U. S. opinion, is of purely theoretical importance, at least for
the time being; basically it means that the manufacture of atomic weapons is not beyond the resources of
a medium-sized nation—a fact already obvious and
destined to become even more so with the spread of
atomic technology. If industrialization and the popu-
larization of nuclear science continue at their present
pace, by the end of the century several dozen nations
will be able to produce nuclear explosives if they so
desire, and at a cost certainly below that of TNT in
terms of yield per ton. But possession of a few bombs
is not the same as possession of a deterrent, let alone
a retaliatory capability. Invulnerable delivery vehicles
capable of penetrating enemy defenses are at present inordinately expensive and, unlike bombs, tend
quickly to grow obsolete. Therefore the sole legitimate

conclusion that can be drawn from this study is one rather self-evident idea: the growth of the gross national product, a fairly general phenomenon at present, will within the next few decades permit almost any industrialized country as well as several still underdeveloped ones to acquire some weapons of mass destruction without having to raise the percentage ratio of their national defense budget in relation to national income.

France spends, for example, at present about 20 billion francs (4 billion dollars), for defense. At an annual growth rate of 5 per cent the national product will have increased more than fourfold over the next thirty years. If the rate drops to 4 per cent, it will take an additional ten years to reach the same point. But in any case a budget of 16 billion dollars, or four times the present amount, though still not exceeding one third of the present U. S. budget, would in all likelihood make possible the acquisition of a substantial retaliatory capability. In short, while the thesis of progressive equalization by the end of the century, with second-class powers having a real retaliatory capability even against the major powers, is far from proved, neither can it be disproved.[4]

The British study considers only nine countries as present candidates for nuclear power: Britain, France, Canada, Germany, China, India, Switzerland, Sweden and Israel. Other countries are omitted, either because they lack the requisite means or because they have shown no interest. I would also exclude Canada, determined not to move in that particular direction for

[4] The uncertainty relates to weapons technology and above all to delivery systems and defenses some decades hence.

psychological reasons that are partly a mask for political ones. Canada was reluctant to stockpile nuclear
arms on Canadian territory; in fact, Diefenbaker's
Conservative government refused categorically. But
Canada's co-operation is vital to the air defense system of the North American continent; Soviet bombers,
and probably missiles as well, must traverse that country to reach targets located in the United States. Canada cannot and does not want to refuse co-operation,
enabling her to profit from U. S. nuclear power, but
this involves some soul-searching.

Sweden and Switzerland both contemplated acquiring nuclear weapons and may not yet have given up
the idea. But they would acquire them in the context
of a neutrality-oriented diplomacy, with the weapons
intended for territorial defense rather than for retaliation. I fail to see in what way the reinforcement of
Swiss or Swedish neutrality with a few tactical atomic
weapons would add significantly to the instability of
the international system or to the dangers threatening
mankind.

Germany is a different case altogether. Under the
1954 Treaty of Paris the Federal Republic solemnly
forswore atomic, bacteriological and chemical weapons. There are no testing grounds on German territory.
No government in Bonn can afford to disregard the
American veto or the violent Russian reaction bound
to meet any attempt to renege on its promise. In the
present situation any West German demands could
cause tension within the Atlantic Alliance, but could
not add another member to the atomic club.

There remain three problem areas: Asia, with China
and possibly India, in reaction, the Middle East with

Israel and perhaps Egypt, and the two Atlantic powers, Britain and France. These three possibilities do not all have the same implications. The vast majority of Americans, from the President and members of Congress to the man in the street, are spontaneously, unequivocally and with a clear conscience opposed to the spread of atomic weapons; and they passionately oppose the proliferation of these diabolical instruments not out of self-interest alone, but for the sake of mankind as a whole. During a visit to Washington in 1963, when I was introduced by one of President Kennedy's close advisers to some friends, he whispered with an apologetic smile that I was "in favor of the dissemination of atomic weapons," as though alluding to a wholly incomprehensible aberration on the part of an otherwise quite sane human being. I am not in favor of the dissemination of atomic weapons as such; but I am struck by the fact that Americans, even those least given to hypocrisy, do not feel bothered by the interpretation to which their attitude lends itself in the eyes of everyone else. If they are worried now about polluting the atmosphere, the fact remains that such scruples did not inhibit them as long as they felt it necessary to enlarge their own arsenal. Why, then, should others be more considerate?

What are the arguments that rationally justify the American policy? The first is the increased danger of an accident, either technological or diplomatic. The argument contains a measure of truth, but just how much is hard to determine. It is possible that novice members of the atomic club would be less careful, either because of scientific incompetence or because they need to cut corners for reasons of economy. But even assuming that accidents may happen,[5] the consequences would still be confined to the countries directly concerned; it would take an overdose of morbid fantasy to visualize the explosion of a single bomb setting off a world-wide chain of disasters.

Another reason given is that small powers, once they have the bomb, are liable to drag the big ones into an all-out war against their will. This fear is also not wholly without a basis in fact; but here again the American tendency is vastly to exaggerate the dangers of dissemination for the United States and disregard the dangers, real or imagined, to the smaller powers. Americans reason that if a bomb were to drop on New York today, they would know that it was launched by the Soviet Union; tomorrow they could no longer be equally certain and might perhaps unjustly accuse their chief opponent. I find it hard to believe that this scenario bears any resemblance to reality as it will shape up some twenty or thirty years from now or that the United States will then have no way of determining the point of origin of a missile. I readily admit that the risk of catalytic war between major powers is bound to increase if several dozen countries possess nuclear weapons and delivery vehicles, but I doubt if the three sets of present candidates—China-India, Israel-Egypt, and France-Britain—contribute substantially to this danger.

The Middle East is the one region where intervention of atomic weapons on either or both sides would fatally aggravate tensions, for two conclusive reasons. For one, Israel is a small country in close proximity to

[5] The peaceful uses of atomic energy also present the danger of accidents.

Egypt, whose cities in turn are of major importance; this would make for a highly unstable situation in that the advantage of a pre-emptive strike would be enormous and quite possibly decisive. Furthermore, the stakes in a conflict between Israel and the Arab countries are part and parcel either of the defense or of the reconquest of the land itself, so that wiping out the entire population now occupying the territory would in no way be incompatible with the aims of one of the belligerents. When it comes to imposing a Carthaginian peace, the atomic weapon constitutes a supremely efficient instrument, since extermination of the enemy can precede victory. If there is one area in the world where the big powers have an obligation to block the introduction of nuclear arms, it is certainly the Middle East. Israel and Egypt both signed the partial test ban. Though both sides have missiles, no outside country will for the time being supply warheads, the manufacture of which in turn requires time, money and outlawed tests.

But however great and perhaps fatal the danger to which Israel and Egypt would expose themselves by introducing nuclear components into their present arms race, it would once again take a fertile imagination to see the Big Two dragged into a holocaust by the possible insanity of Middle Eastern nations. In fact, it seems to me almost certain that once nuclear arms make their appearance in the area, a diplomatic subsystem would automatically detach itself from the global system. The Big Two are less and less able to impose their will upon the small states because the threat of extermination as a measure of constraint is far too disproportionately outrageous to be plausible;

but they could convey to one another their intent of non-intervention, or at least they could renounce their promises of unconditional assistance the moment enemies, allies or uncommitted nations come into possession of atomic weapons.

China's acquisition of an atomic force would probably lead to consequences that are distinctly unpleasant to contemplate. India might respond by manufacturing bombs in turn; as a result, the Asian subsystem, while not cutting all its ties to the global system, would be much less dependent on it. One of the causes of the Moscow-Peking quarrel was Soviet refusal fully to support the action against Quemoy and Matsu in 1958. As of 1964, the Chinese-Russian mutual assistance treaty is still in force; China, after a fashion, continues to be covered against nuclear threats by her Russian ally. But this would definitely cease the moment China tried to protect herself by means of her own. In other words, the spread of atomic weapons would encourage a breakdown in the unity of the global system and would attenuate the bipolarity that the thermonuclear duopoly is now maintaining in one specific and narrow sector of international relations.

No one knows precisely where the Chinese stand with their atomic program, but the disorganization of the Chinese economy after the failure of the "great leap forward," as well as French estimates as to the time required for the production of thermonuclear bombs, would make it seem likely that while the first atomic explosions may take place soon, some ten to fifteen years will probably pass before China can produce thermonuclear bombs, fifteen to twenty before she has both a minimal quantity of bombs and modern delivery vehicles such as supersonic bombers or ballistic missiles.

In the initial phase, with China an atomic power in much the same sense as France, the change will be chiefly psychological. In the eyes of the underdeveloped countries China will seem to have repeated the Russian miracle and to have raised herself by her own efforts and sacrifices to the level of an advanced industrial civilization. One may also imagine a different reaction and expect China, guilty of having polluted the atmosphere after the Moscow test ban, to stand morally condemned by the representatives of the non-aligned nations, all of whom are so passionately articulate in their invectives against the French tests. But I am rather inclined to believe that the countries of Latin America, Africa and Asia will find it in their hearts to forgive China what they cannot forgive France and that Peking will be hailed for the same technical feat that makes France a criminal.

Regardless of whether the Peking-Moscow mutual assistance pact is formally abrogated or not, if the Soviet Union keeps aloof, China's position vis-à-vis the United States will not be improved by the acquisition of a few atom bombs. In a way, the European situation of 1946–53 will be re-enacted, with the United States invulnerable and all of China exposed to the American force. On the other hand, China would have conventional as well as atomic forces, enabling her to strike blows against America's allies. From the European precedent we know that such a situation implies a certain degree of stability, despite tensions set up within the coalition between the protector country, sheltered by distance from a direct attack, and the

protected countries, liable to reprisals because of proximity.

If China eventually becomes a first-rate thermonuclear power able to maintain a balance of sorts with
the other members of the atomic club, she would in
the long run, perhaps some twenty years from now, be
tempted by the extremist doctrine of the atomic shield
and the conventional sword. Given her military superiority over all Asian countries except the Soviet Union, it would be quite enough for her to paralyze the
thermonuclear forces of the other big powers in order
to impose her rule upon all her neighbors; she has, in
fact, started to do just that even before establishing
the balance at a higher level. But beyond these generalities, there is no point in hazarding predictions;
much depends on relations between Moscow and Peking twenty years hence. A reconciliation between
Khrushchev and Mao is out of the question, and so,
most likely, is restoration of perfect unity within the
communist camp; this, however, does not mean that
the conflict is bound to explode into a full-fledged fight
to the death over Russia's Asian empire.

Finally, a few things remain to be said about France
and Britain, the two atomic powers within the Atlantic
Alliance. I have already discussed them at some length
in previous chapters and will here confine myself to
some remarks based on the preceding analysis. The
proposition that alliances are incompatible with atomic
weapons—because deterrence on behalf of another
country is no longer plausible—seems to me paradoxical as well as fallacious, at least for the next twenty
years. It is paradoxical to suppose that political-mili-
tary units tend to shrink in inverse ratio to the growing

destructive power of weapons. There is no precedent for assuming that the major powers will fall back on their own territories instead of attempting to reach an accommodation providing for reciprocal respect of their vital interests.

As long as no European country possesses a genuine thermonuclear force of its own—even Britain, relying on the U. S. warning and detection system, is far from it—only the United States will be able to offset the Soviet deterrent. For the next fifteen years a European deterrent would meet not even the minimal requirements for balance; moreover its existence remains highly improbable, since it would necessitate the co-operation of Britain, which prefers to co-operate with the United States. A genuine federation of European states is as yet nowhere in sight.

The Atlantic Alliance is endangered by a conflict somewhat analogous to the Chinese-Russian rift—the refusal of Gaullist France to respect what in Washington is called solidarity and in Paris, subservience. France, as President Kennedy said on the eve of signing the Moscow test ban, is an atomic power and could qualify for American aid, subject to one condition that Macmillan's Britain accepted but de Gaulle's France refused: integration of the force into the Atlantic deterrent. True, the so-called multinational formula reserves the right of withdrawal, but it implies the intent of joint strategy and diplomacy to begin with, an intent General de Gaulle castigates as a form of submission and counters by appealing to the will for independence. The resulting conflict is insoluble as long as each side persists in its rigid attitude, but it will probably not ultimately wreck the Alliance altogether because the scope and strength of the French deterrent in the next ten years will remain much too insignificant to arouse serious American fears that the United States would be dragged into a war against the Soviet Union contrary to American interests and intentions.

In short, what really imperils alliances is assertions of independence by the protégés rather than gradual weakening of the protection offered by the protectors. The big powers do not refuse to assume responsibility for the protection of vital interests beyond their borders, but they also do not intend to expose themselves to responses provoked by possible initiatives on the part of their allies. For the time being, *the big powers insist on making their own monopoly of operational command a condition of alliance.* A non-Gaullist or perhaps even a Gaullist France will sooner or later accept a compromise along the lines of the multinational force. If she refuses to do so, she will make it that much harder for the Alliance to function without therefore necessarily provoking a complete break,[6] because for the next ten or fifteen years the French deterrent will be too weak to inspire serious fears in either Moscow or Washington, even as a "trigger."

The conclusion, contrary to all fashionable theories, is that alliances are in effect threatened in the thermonuclear age, but more by big-power demands than by the actual dangers to which the small countries are liable. A big power will not form an alliance whose purpose is to deter aggression by the threat of nuclear retaliation unless it retains exclusive control of strategy.

[6] At least the military controversy will not cause the break, though other purely political reasons may do so.

To a certain extent this disposes of the argument about the weakened credibility of deterrence as a result of increased U. S. vulnerability; *integration reaffirms the unity of the coalition, but at the same time it also affirms the loss of military independence on the part of states sovereign in theory.*

I lack the requisite competence to predict the consequences of technological progress, or what I prefer to call the qualitative arms race, in the coming ten or twenty years. In part, the outcome of this race will be decided by the doctrines and intentions of the Big Two.

At the moment, as we have seen, the United States—if we are to believe the American experts—possesses the greater number of missiles, and they are better protected and less vulnerable than the Russian long-range missiles, although the latter are also in the process of being hardened. The Russians, on the other hand, have a large number of medium-range missiles aimed at Western Europe; they have also tested more powerful bombs (among them one of 57 megatons). American experts have opposed U. S. participation in a superbomb race. According to Camille Rougeron, these superbombs involve certain high-altitude explosion techniques whose main effect would be thermal, covering thousands of square miles.[7] Pentagon technicians apparently do not subscribe to these notions; one of them, to whom I submitted this problem, told me that he did not know whether the idea of ultra-high-altitude explosions of superbombs originated with the Russians, but that he did not consider the thermal effects of bombs in the range of several

[7] In the Bikini test, dangerous radiation extended over 7000 square miles.

dozen megatons to be particularly destructive compared to blast and radiation effects. The radioactive fallout seemed to him vastly more dangerous to civilian targets.[8]

Secretary McNamara himself is on record as having admitted that U. S. strategic counterforce capability will continue to decline as Russian missiles become hardened and more missile-equipped submarines become operational. Whatever advantages Russia or the United States can derive either from improvement in the volume-to-power ratio of thermonuclear warheads[9] or from faster interceptors or higher-altitude bombers, a really substantial change can be brought about only by a technical breakthrough that would yield the beneficiary an offensive or defensive capability sufficient if not to deprive the adversary of all retaliatory capability, then at least to create a substantial imbalance leading inevitably to his marked inferiority in any test of will.

The possibilities along these lines as they appear at present to one who is not a technician seem to lie in three general areas: (1) modification in the relationship between shell and armor—i.e., the number of missiles required to destroy a hardened missile, or the probability with which bombers can penetrate ground-to-air missile defense lines; (2) the perfection of anti-missile missiles, and (3) substantial progress in civilian defense.

The number of missiles required to destroy a hard-

[8] Nevertheless, Secretary McNamara admitted during the Senate hearings that superbombs could be used in high-altitude explosions to start conflagrations over vast areas.

[9] The Americans are ahead in small bombs and the Russians in large ones.

ened missile depends, as we have seen, on the explosive power of the warhead, the accuracy of the shot, and the resistance of the armor (concrete reinforcement of the silos). The figures mentioned here and there are relatively meaningless as long as we lack the data on which they are based. Technological progress over the last few years seems to have favored attack over defense,[10] with circular error probability amounting to very few miles even over very large distances and with improvements in the volume-to-power ratio making it possible to increase the power of warheads for any given missile. But mobile ramps, submarines, surface vessels and air-to-ground missiles tend in the opposite direction.

Everything known at this time about both the Russian and the American programs would lead one to expect the balance to be maintained for the next ten to fifteen years, at least as regards the relationship between shell and armor. The Soviet superbombs, whether intended to act by blast, heat or radiation, seem designed for countercity rather than counterforce strategy.[11] The Minuteman, on the other hand, is designed for a different strategy, but its warhead has a power of only one or two megatons; if the Russians are seriously worried about this weapon, they should have no trouble reinforcing the armor of their launching ramps to the point where the increased number of missiles required to destroy each silo will reduce

[10] More accurately, the strategic counterforce capability, by increasing the risk of destruction to non-hardened missiles.

[11] Not all U. S. experts share this opinion. Some believe that a very large bomb could destroy an average of two missiles. Above all, a blanket of superbombs could destroy the communications and command networks.

U. S. counterforce capability to a level compatible with
Russian security. In any event, there remain the missile-equipped submarines, impossible to track with
presently available techniques, and the intermediate-
range missiles aimed at targets along the western
fringe of the Eurasian land mass—that is, all the cities
of Western Europe.

Aside from weapons yet unknown, the one technological revolution conceivable would be an effective
defense against missiles. The Russians have displayed
on this subject a sanguine optimism, striking in its contrast to the pessimism expressed by President Kennedy
in August 1963. M. Rougeron explains this contrast
by recourse to his pet theory: distinguishing between
decoy and missile requires an atmosphere of such density that it is impossible when dealing with missiles designed to explode at high altitudes, while techniques
effective against the relatively weak Polaris-type missiles can be devised.[12] Perfection of anti-missile missiles by one side, though it would still not make the
defense one hundred per cent effective—especially
since the other side could conceivably resort to different types of vehicles such as bombers, satellites, and
air-to-ground missiles—would nonetheless result in a
substantial advantage, with political consequences difficult to foresee.

And finally, the side initiating a vast civil defense
program would be ahead to some extent, in its ability
to absorb punishment. Neither has constructed nor, it
seems, ever seriously contemplated the construction
of underground shelters in which urban populations

[12] High-altitude explosions of superbombs may also eventually
be used to destroy missiles in flight.

could survive thermonuclear explosions and wait out the two or three weeks required for the elimination of radioactivity. In the United States even a very modest program of mass or family fallout shelters received little support in Congress and has not made much headway. Indifference to civil defense is rationalized by the "hostage theory": by leaving its population unprotected, each side is manifesting its peaceful intent in a concrete and incontrovertible manner. As long as civil defense continues to be neglected, the common interest of the Big Two in not fighting each other will far outweigh the stakes in any conflict.[13] The inclusion of civil defense in the qualitative arms race is, in fact, unlikely at the moment. For the time being the Russians will continue to manufacture superbombs which they no longer need to test; the Americans are relying on large numbers of missiles with warheads of one or several megatons and intend in the next few years to scrap first their B-47 bombers, then their B-52s and ultimately perhaps even the supersonic B-58. The end of the role of bombers as strategic delivery vehicles is in sight, but fighters, fighter-bombers or interceptors, probably with vertical take-off, will be put into operation instead.

The major goal of the qualitative arms race in both Russia and America is the anti-missile missile (and possibly also the military exploitation of outer space). After picking up speed in 1961–62, it seems to have slowed down as a result of prevailing U. S. concepts

[13] This has never seemed to me altogether convincing. In that case, why not guarantee the enemy invulnerability and penetration for his reprisal weapons? There are, in fact, simpler explanations for the reluctance to embark on extensive civil defense programs.

and Khrushchev's apparent receptivity to their general tenor.

The advisers chosen by President Kennedy and Secretary McNamara included more civilians, college professors, and specialists in nuclear strategy than have ever served in any previous administration, and the diplomacy as well as strategy of the present government is profoundly influenced by the manner of thinking that most of these men have in common, despite their widely divergent views on vital issues.

In 1961 the Kennedy Administration vacillated between two schematic models: stability based on reciprocal invulnerability of deterrents, and strategic counterforce capability, supposedly made necessary by the geographic structure of the Atlantic Alliance and by the cover the United States had to provide in unusual circumstances for many allied countries. At any rate, orders went out immediately to increase the number and invulnerability of reprisal weapons, before the election slogan of the famous "missile gap" had been forgotten. But in January 1963 McNamara announced the progressive and probably continuing decline in counterforce capability. Even so, the Administration does not fully accept the thesis of perfect stability between invulnerable deterrents; if they did, they would have to expand their conventional armaments and bar the possibility of escalation.

Their concept is a different one altogether. They hope to convince Khrushchev that on the one hand threats or force of arms will get him nowhere, and that on the other the Big Two have a common interest in not destroying one another, in preventing the proliferation of nuclear arms, and in not aggravating the dangers threatening both countries by accelerating the arms race; the historic conflict between the so-called socialist governments and those referred to as capitalist must not be decided by war unto death. During the first two years of his term Kennedy had no apparent success in his attempts at conversion or persuasion; the Soviets conducted more atmospheric tests than ever before, and even Stalin never took such a risk as Khrushchev did when he installed missiles in Cuba. The disarmament talks never seemed more futile.

Then, in the summer of 1963 with the signing of the Moscow test ban treaty, came Moscow's first positive reaction to Kennedy's political concepts. It was not that the treaty as such, literally interpreted, had any significance beyond that of a moratorium on atmospheric tests that the Big Two could have declared unilaterally; but Khrushchev's language and the ideological break between Moscow and Peking seemed to indicate that the distance between Soviet and American leaders was growing smaller and that both teams tended to interpret the formula of peaceful co-existence in pretty much the same sense. Although the Big Two continue to be enemies on the ideological plane as well as on the level of power relations, they are bent on avoiding armed confrontation wherever possible and, in any event, are determined not to use their most awesome weapons.

To what extent will the qualitative arms race slow down? Will Khrushchev come to agree with some of the President's advisers that the stockpiling of arms leads to growing insecurity? Or will he or his successor revert tomorrow to pressure tactics, brandish 100-megaton bombs, and boast about the efficacy of anti-missile

missiles? Eighteen years of experience have taught us
not to mistake the periodic succession of deliberately
induced Soviet thaws and freezes for the end of a conflict that time alone, with the aid of new and different
clashes, can bring to a definite conclusion.

Inevitably, the Russian-American rapprochement favored by thermonuclear weapons exerts an influence
also on the political relations between the Big Two,
but the latter cannot yet be completely harmonious.
The men in the Kremlin cannot forswear their faith in
world revolution without revealing themselves as re-
visionists, thus proving Mao's point. Where no serious
risk of war exists, the contest between Peking and
Moscow might assume the shape of a verbally intran-
sigent rivalry inspired by ideological fervor. It may
conceivably be more difficult to reach a compromise in
any given area of the world with a divided communist
camp than it would have been with a unified one. But
if the Big Two should openly proclaim their solidarity
against war and their relative indifference to the political aspirations of their respective allies, thus allaying
some fears, founded or unfounded, mankind would
come to see the rivalry between them in a different
light and judge the issues between them by different
criteria.

Will the two blocs as now constituted resist this subtle but profound change of climate?

The rapprochement between Russia and the United
States will be judged by their respective allies in terms
of its effects upon themselves. In Eastern Europe the
so-called satellites have already regained greater autonomy as a result of the Peking-Moscow split. When
the Rumanians have cause to feel dissatisfied with the

division of labor as provided by COMECON, Bucha-
rest newspapers publish the Twenty-five Point thesis
of the Chinese Communist Party and thus advertise
their neutrality between the opposing centers of Marxism-Leninism. But there are two reasons why no genuine opposition to the Kremlin's *strategy* can exist in
Eastern Europe. For one, the ruling elites must rely
upon the Soviet empire as the necessary source of their
power, and for another, the Kremlin's present goal
is perpetuation of the *status quo*, a goal in which all
governments of Eastern Europe must of necessity concur. Matters are different on the other side of the line.

In the West, the *de facto* territorial settlement imposed upon Europe in 1945 by the Russian and American armies is tolerated rather than accepted. Spokesmen for both blocs swear by their different gods that
they will not resort to force in order to change the face
of the map or overthrow governments, but at the same
time Western statesmen assert that they will not legally
or morally recognize the German Democratic Republic. The combination of non-recognition and abstention
from the use of force is not impossible but tends to
become increasingly more uncomfortable as the détente progresses. It is easy for the Soviets to denounce
these contradictions—by what miracle does the West
want to reconstitute German unity if it bars recourse
to force of arms? In other words, the military stability
in Europe, which could easily be strengthened by reducing the armed forces stationed on either side of the
line and introducing some limited inspection, itself *involves* or *supposes* political stability. The goal of the
West until now has been the greatest possible military
stability in spite of political instability, that is, in spite

of the manifest desire for change in one of the camps. The enemies of the status quo, chiefly leaders of the Federal Republic, rightly fear that any agreements aimed at military stabilization will in the long run bring about political stabilization as well.

A different strategy for the West and for the Federal Republic would have been conceivable. Since no one is either able or willing to overthrow the Soviet regimes or drive Russian troops out of Eastern Europe by force of arms or the threat thereof, might it not be better to seize the initiative, frankly to accept relations with the satellite states, including the German Democratic Republic, and to weaken these regimes by the exposure to Western influence that would inevitably result? In Europe, the Western type of regime is the one most closely identified with the aspirations of the people and with the trend of social evolution, sometimes called the "meaning of history." Soviet-style regimes outside Russia are fragile and synthetic creations; once the threat of Russian armies is removed they will be liberalized much faster than Russia herself; once the barriers erected by Soviet and Atlantic armies are down, the breach between the two halves of Europe will be healed.

Perhaps the Federal Republic will some day reverse the course of its diplomacy and, without changing its objective—the absorption of the so-called Democratic Republic in a united and genuinely democratic Germany—seek to attain its goal by stressing political flexibility rather than by a military freeze. But until such reversal takes place, the détente between Russia and the United States that has already contributed to the split between Moscow and Peking will inevitably arouse a certain amount of tension between Washington on the one hand and Paris and Bonn on the other—between Washington and Paris because of the nuclear aspirations of Gaullist France, and between Washington and Bonn because of Washington's consent, implicit in its quest for military stability, to the political status quo.

By way of summarizing this exploratory outline, we might start with the fact that the qualitative arms race will continue in spite of the perhaps temporary suspension of atmospheric tests; technological progress in weaponry, silos and delivery vehicles is self-perpetuating and cannot be arrested at any given point except by a joint decision of both major powers, implemented by an effective inspection system to guarantee observation of the agreement. Since such an agreement will almost certainly not come to pass, the arms race will continue, although not necessarily at top speed. Both the United States and the Soviet Union consider the race exceedingly costly. In the teeth of violent criticism Secretary McNamara has gone farther than any of his predecessors in a program of selective emphasis and elimination among the various weapons systems and, banking on the Polaris and Minuteman missiles for 1965–70 and beyond, has successively dropped the Skybolt project, long-range air-to-ground missiles, the atomic airplane engine, and even the RS-70, which by the end of the decade was to have replaced the B-52 and B-58. The latter two planes are still operational at present but are scheduled to be scrapped or put on reserve as replacements become available. The Johnson Administration seems to lean toward the thesis (ex-

pounded for some years now by the most pacifistically
inclined specialists) that the United States should consider unilateral measures of arms control,[14] and that
the Soviet Union will respond in kind, because such
measures conform to the interests of both sides.

Henceforth, in spite of replacing bombers with missiles, in spite of heavier, more numerous and more accurate missiles, in spite of faster interceptors or fighter-
bombers with vertical take-off ability, neither side is
likely to acquire a decisive superiority. That would
come about only in case of a very serious error in the
choice of weapons systems by one side or the unilateral
perfection of either a missile defense or of an offensive
weapon so powerful as to obliterate the enemy's entire reprisal capability in a single blow. Although technically none of these hypotheses can be altogether excluded, it would seem far more likely that whatever
advantage either major power possesses at any given
moment would not be sufficiently decisive to tempt it
into running the risk of all-out war (the more so in
view of the fact that if either side regains a substantial
first-strike counterforce capability, it must once again
fear its rival's pre-emptive strike).

If the Big Two were alone in the world, they would
react to this upper-level stability in one of two ways:
either by reducing any lag in conventional arms, as
the Americans have done, or by preventing all direct
confrontations between armed forces of the two countries, as the Russians seem to be doing. In other words,
assuming a growing stability between Russian and
American deterrents, either the dissymmetry between

[14] For example, the reduction of fissionable materials and the
scrapping of obsolete bombers.

the American theory of chess and the Russian theory of poker will continue, or else the Big Two may both adopt the same doctrine, Russian or American; a third possibility is some sort of combination, accompanied by a political détente.

In terms of abstract analysis the most plausible hypothesis is Soviet acceptance of the American conceptual scheme. Escalation to extremes is becoming more and more improbable because of its catastrophic implications for all concerned; therefore the margin for subatomic operations tends to grow. Russians and Americans, playing chess against one another, would run ever greater risks of local hostilities while trying to reduce the danger of all-out war, but they would end up paradoxically increasing that danger once they smugly came to feel that they had both grasped to perfection the rules jointly agreed upon.

I asked one of Secretary McNamara's advisers whether he thought that Soviet leaders subscribed to American strategic doctrine. After referring me to *Soviet Military Strategy* by V. D. Sokolovsky,[15] which unquestionably suggests a negative reply, he added that in his opinion there was little to indicate that the Russians "meant to play the game our way." But he added that even if they do, they may for obvious reasons prefer to conceal it; and if they have not yet thought of it at all, they probably will. Clearly there are situations in which to do so would be in their own best interest.

[15] Two English translations of the first Russian edition have been published, one by Praeger and the other by Prentice-Hall. In the second Russian edition, as yet untranslated, the authors seem to exhibit greater understanding of the American doctrine and less hostility toward it.

This answer contains one incontrovertible element, and another that is at once incontrovertible and paradoxical. Russian strategists have served notice that any war between the two power blocs would be total from the day it started, and that they would strike indiscriminately at the economic and human resources as well as the armed forces of the enemy both in Europe and in the United States. Nothing, however, proves that in the hour of truth they would act upon these publicly proclaimed intentions. The idea of limitation, although rejected in theory, may well come to be accepted in practice when the fatal decision has to be made. The American strategists are therefore justified in not entirely discarding this possibility, however slim they may consider it to be.

The proposition I refer to as at once incontrovertible and paradoxical is that the Russians, if they do intend to observe the American rules of the game, have obvious reasons for disguising all such intentions. But if this is true of the Soviet Union, why not also of the United States? Why should the Americans reveal their moves ahead of time while the Russians keep theirs secret? One answer is that the United States is unable to refrain from talking and can create an impression of mystery and mystification only by means of telling all, and then some. The second is that the party diplomatically on the defensive increases the efficacy of its deterrent by stressing the multiplicity of potential responses available. A third and perhaps most meaningful answer would be that each doctrine breeds its dialectical antithesis in the thinking of the opponent. The Russians, according to their public statements, will not take seriously the speculations of college professors and reject all intermediate stages between the initial explosion of tactical atomic weapons and the all-out use of every atomic and thermonuclear weapon available. In the abstract the Americans are obviously right; it is downright irrational to cling to the all-or-nothing alternative if the "all" involves the atomic death of millions of people. Nevertheless, if the Russians regard this alternative as a means of frightening U. S. leaders, they will not openly renounce it no matter what they may think of it in private.

There remains the fact that the Russians' geographic situation, including the ability to maneuver along inner lines of communication, and local superiority at many points along the line of demarcation, will tend to give the Soviet Union an advantage in the American game once their own deterrent becomes invulnerable. Will U. S. strategists thereupon take up the Russian doctrine if the men in Moscow adopt American theories? They may not go quite that far; but they would be forced to stress the possibility of escalation once the Russians emphasize the feasibility of avoiding it. In other words, the Russians would have just as obvious reasons to publicize as to conceal their conversion to the tactics of chess but this conversion might, in turn, force the Americans, if not to adopt their enemy's present doctrine, at least to shift the accent within their own scheme so as to emphasize the risk of escalation[16] rather than the chances of avoiding it.

These exercises in dialectic illustrate the essential nature of the game, the double necessity for each to leave his rival in doubt as to the way he is going to

[16] Which is precisely what they are doing in Berlin, just as they did during the massive-retaliation phase.

play the game and also to prepare in advance the lines of communication between them for use in the hour of truth. Soviet conversion to the doctrine of flexibility would add to the dangers, but given the enormity of the consequences, the players—regardless of how improbable a stroke of really bad luck may be—will include in their calculations not only those decisions an ideal strategist would deem rational, nor yet only those that would appear rational by the standards of the officially adopted doctrine, but also those that rashness, loss of nerve, or sheer insanity may inspire in men of flesh and blood. Barring technological breakthroughs in weapons systems, the relationship between the Big Two in the next ten to twenty years will evolve from a complex dialectic, with neither wholly able to predict in advance the other's conduct and with each reserving, right up to the very last moment, the chance to influence the other in order to avert the worst. The officially proclaimed thaw may perhaps add an element of reconciliation; the game will not be completely stopped, but rather suspended, and moves considered too dangerous will by joint agreement be avoided.

This game now being played by Russia and the United States with growing confidence in their respective mastery of it may be spoiled by the arrival on the scene of some new players. Ten or fifteen years from now China will in all probability have become an atomic power, unable to strike at the American mainland but capable of partly immobilizing the American deterrent by threats against Asian states linked to the West. Such a situation would make war between today's Big Two even less likely than now, because the

Soviet Union would separate itself from China as the latter acquired the means for an independent strategy.

In the West, the French atomic program has a triple function, or at least it is being justified by three arguments: to prevent the two extra-European states from having a monopoly of atomic technology, to take out insurance against the unforeseeable future and against the long-range trend in U. S. policy, and lastly, to acquire the prestige that attaches to membership in the atomic club along with the ability to influence American strategy. Co-operation along British lines, even at the price of integration, is in no way incompatible with any of these functions. What it does preclude, however, are pretensions to a wholly independent diplomacy and strategy, which, I am aware, are General de Gaulle's main concerns. But in this respect I am afraid that his philosophy derives merely from nostalgia for the kind of independence vanished with "the good old days."

In the next fifteen years no independent national deterrent will have a security value equal to the presence of American troops on European soil and to the strength of the American commitment that results from it. If tomorrow or the day after a further rapprochement between the Big Two or the growing rift between Moscow and Peking progressively reduces the chances of war between NATO and the Soviet empire, a revision of the Atlantic Pact resulting in increased autonomy for either a small or a greater Europe may become a distinct possibility. Under such circumstances any French force would be at the complete disposal of the French Government, even if in the meantime it had been under NATO command, just as the British force remains at the disposal of Her Majesty's Government if changes in the situation so require.

The idea of an independent deterrent in the service of a national diplomacy is rooted in illusions. French policy in Africa or Latin America is fully independent of American influence, with or without a deterrent. The same holds true at the economic level, where the influence of French diplomacy stands to increase in proportion to the growth in cohesiveness of the Common Market. In this context the military concepts of General de Gaulle, which are not shared by any of our Common Market partners, tend to detract from French influence more than they add to it. As to strategic autonomy in the traditional sense of the term, the ability to make sovereign decisions concerning war and peace, during the next fifteen years this will be neither feasible nor desirable. The farther France moves from the Alliance and the more capable she seems of the fatal initiative, the less willing Americans will be to commit themselves. And, to repeat in the nineteen-seventies the cause of French security will be best served if American commitment is supplemented by a French force that does not provoke withdrawal of transatlantic troops and keeps the choice of a future course open.

Those who would like to see the Atlantic Alliance replaced by an alliance of the traditional type, with each member free to use atomic weapons as it sees fit and able to rely on automatic support from its allies, have simply failed to grasp the most elementary facts of the new diplomacy shaped by nuclear explosives. What thermonuclear weapons have rendered obsolete are not alliances as such but alliances of the traditional type. The big nations are still able to protect the small ones but will not consent to do so if the latter claim the prerogative of initiating thermonuclear disaster. Alliances will either evolve toward communities or else dissolve altogether; they will certainly not revert to their pre-atomic prototypes.

Fifteen years ago French and other European nationalists failed to understand that the Marshall Plan would eventually lead to the economic independence, rather than the enslavement of France and of Europe. Those same nationalists today refuse to understand that the same holds true in the nuclear sphere. Military independence, assuming that it will remain a goal in future, presupposes a phase of co-operation with the United States during which French leaders will have to learn the strange game of brandishing threats never to be carried out. They will discover the advantages of a unified strategy for as long a period as independent forces are both too weak and too vulnerable to permit any but the insane poker game of massive retaliation.

The goal, or course, is a Europe fully restored and pacified at last by awareness of its common cultural heritage and by the end of ideological conflicts. But a Western Europe that is not sufficiently armed to offset Soviet power but too much so to retain full American protection would lead neither to peace through equilibrium nor to peace through reconciliation. The men of Moscow would be much less likely to reach agreement with a Europe in which the German Federal Republic is predominant than with the United States. The reunification of Eastern and Western Europe requires a détente between the two blocs rather than a loosening of the ties between the two segments of the Atlantic Alliance.

The term "national ambition" is not devoid of grandeur, but France needs a goal worthy of her ambition. The free choice between war and peace, essence of sovereignty in the traditional sense of the word, no longer has the same meaning now that the choice of war implies or could imply the annihilation of the nation itself. Military independence may possibly remain a value, but certainly not a supreme goal. Integration within an alliance is both morally and materially preferable to isolation so long as it contributes to the chances for peace. The threat of recourse to war remains an indispensable weapon in the jungle of diplomacy, but the common interest of all players, enemies and allies, requires their not carrying out their threats. It is therefore vital that a nation's efforts to lessen its dependence on a protector shall not compromise its own security, the strength of the alliance, or the safety of mankind as a whole.

There will always be room for argument about the best method of reconciling the desire of some members of the Alliance for autonomy and the demands of the others for integration. But solutions, always short of perfection and always temporary, can be worked out only by avoiding the pitfalls of living either in the too-distant past or in the too-distant future. The traditional type of alliance is obsolete for thermonuclear powers; such nations will not commit themselves on behalf of allies demanding full freedom of action. And any security that possession of a national deterrent may offer small or medium-sized nations would seem to lie far beyond the present horizon of history.

To value the power of independent choice between war and peace above national security may once have been a sign of greatness. But I do not believe that in the thermonuclear age this should be considered an appropriate goal for the national ambition of a nation such as France.